Brain-Compatible Activities for Mathematics

Grades 4-5

Brain-Compatible
Activities for
Mathematics

Grades 4-5

David A. Sousa

CORWIN
A SAGE Company

For information:

Corwin
A SAGE Company
2455 Teller Road
Thousand Oaks, California 91320
(800) 233-9936
Fax: (800) 417-2466
www.corwinpress.com

SAGE Ltd.
1 Oliver's Yard
55 City Road
London EC1Y 1SP
United Kingdom

SAGE India Pvt. Ltd.
B 1/I 1 Mohan Cooperative Industrial Area
Mathura Road, New Delhi 110 044
India

SAGE Asia-Pacific Pte. Ltd.
33 Pekin Street #02-01
Far East Square
Singapore 048763

Printed in the United States of America.

Library of Congress Cataloging-in-Publication Data

Sousa, David A.
Brain-compatible activities for mathematics, Grades 4-5/David A. Sousa.
    p. cm.
Includes bibliographical references and index.
ISBN 978-1-4129-6787-7 (pbk.)
    1. Mathematics—Study and teaching (Elementary)—Activity programs. I. Title.

QA135.6.S5662 2010
372.7—dc22   2009037008

This book is printed on acid-free paper.

09 10 11 12 13 10 9 8 7 6 5 4 3 2 1

Managing Editor:	Cathy Hernandez
Executive Editor:	Kathleen Hex
Developmental Writers:	Jeff Sanders, Nancy Sanders, Karen Hall
Developmental Editor:	Christine Hood
Editorial Assistant:	Sarah Bartlett
Production Editor:	Cassandra Margaret Seibel
Copy Editor:	Barbara Corrigan
Typesetter:	C&M Digitals (P) Ltd.
Proofreader:	Sarah J. Duffy
Cover Designer:	Karine Hovsepian
Illustrators:	Mark Mason, Jenny Campbell, Dana Regan, Mary Rojas, Scott Rolfs, Robbie Short, Jamie Smith

Contents

Introduction

Brain-compatible math activities are fun and exciting! These activities are often hands on and involve partners, group work, and class movement, which many students enjoy. Students frequently say that mathematics is difficult for them. Therefore, as an educator, it is your job to choose materials that are likely to be effective in light of current research on how the brain learns mathematics. This book is filled with activities that are centered on brain research and that are structured to maximize the brain's learning potential.

The activities in this book are designed using a brain-compatible lesson plan format. There are nine components of the plan, but not all nine are necessary for every lesson. Those components that are most relevant to the learning objective should be emphasized:

1. anticipatory set,

2. learning objective,

3. purpose,

4. input,

5. modeling,

6. checking for understanding,

7. guided practice,

8. closure, and

9. independent practice.

Each of the components is described in detail in the book titled *How the Brain Learns Mathematics* (Sousa, 2008). Refer to that book for more brain-compatible math research and other teaching strategies. When using the activities in this book, read through the activity first. Then begin preparations for the lesson. It is best to follow the lesson plan format to ensure maximum learning potential. However, meeting the needs of each student in your classroom is always first and foremost. Be flexible to ensure that all students are learning. Last, have fun! These activities may force you to step out of your comfort zone. Embrace the change, and watch your students' brains at work.

PUT IT INTO PRACTICE

How the brain learns is a fascinating and complex process. Advancements in research and technology are helping us understand specifically how the brain learns math and deals with numbers and mathematical relationships. These remarkable findings are improving teaching and learning dramatically. An educator's understanding and applying instructional approaches that are compatible with what cognitive studies tell us will only aid in his or her classroom success.

Some of the recent research discoveries about the brain can and should affect teaching and learning. For example, research tells us that

- creating and using conceptual subitizing patterns help young students develop the abstract number and arithmetic strategies they will need to master counting;
- just as phonemic awareness is a prerequisite to learning phonics and becoming a successful reader, developing number sense is a prerequisite for succeeding in mathematics;
- information is most likely to store if it makes sense and has meaning;
- too often, mathematics instruction focuses on skills, knowledge, and performance but spends little time on reasoning and deep understanding; and
- mathematics can be defined simply as the science of patterns.

A much fuller explanation of these discoveries and their implications for school and the classroom can be found in my book *How the Brain Learns Mathematics* (2008), published by Corwin. This book is designed as a classroom resource to accompany that text. The activities in this book translate the research and strategies for brain-compatible math teaching and learning into practical, successful classroom activities. Some general guidelines provide the framework for these activities:

- Writing is an important component in learning mathematics.
- Studies show that more students are motivated and succeed in classes where teachers use activities that address the various intelligences.
- The use of concrete models for representation of concepts and to help create meaning is beneficial.
- Connecting concepts to the real world creates purpose and meaning. This allows math to seem less abstract.
- Using graphic organizers helps students organize their thinking.
- Solving problems in different ways is beneficial to students.

The activities in this book also are supported by research-based rationale for using particular instructional strategies. These strategies include cooperative learning groups, differentiated instruction, discussion, reflection, movement, manipulatives, visualization, and many others, all of which can increase student motivation and retention of learned concepts.

Scientists continue to explore the inner workings of the brain and will likely continue to discover more and more about learning mathematics. Teachers are challenged to stay current on these new findings, to ensure students are using their brains to the fullest capacity. As we learn more about how the brain learns mathematics we can develop activities like those seen in this book, which will

- aid in teachers' presenting meaningful instruction to students in the classroom,
- ensure that students are staying focused and remembering more of what teachers have presented, and
- make teaching and learning more effective and enjoyable experiences.

Teachers should always continue to help students recognize that the learning of mathematics will not only be helpful in their future but allow them to understand and appreciate the wonders of the world each day.

Links to Focal Points and Standards

CONNECTIONS TO FOCAL POINTS

This chart shows the National Council of Teachers of Mathematics (2008) focal points covered in this book.

Grade 4

Focal Points		Page Numbers
Number and Operations and Algebra: Multiplication and Division	Develop quick recall of multiplication and division facts and fluency with multiplication of whole numbers. Apply understanding of models for multiplication. Analyze and select appropriate strategies for estimate and calculate products.	2, 6, 9, 13, 16
Number and Operations: Fractions and Decimals	Understand decimals as an extension of the base-ten system of writing whole numbers. Use models to identify fractional parts. Make the connection between fractions and decimals. Identify equivalent fractions and compare and order fractions and decimals.	42, 47, 51, 57, 61
Geometry and Measurement	Work with two-dimensional shapes to understand how to identify and measure perimeter and area. Identify and classify different angles. Extend knowledge of symmetry and congruence to encompass transformations and design.	82, 87, 91, 95, 99
Algebra	Continue to identify, describe, and extend numeric patterns involving all operations. Investigate changes in variables and learn to use rules for repeating patterns.	118, 121, 124, 127
Data Analysis	Expand knowledge of and experience with using tools to solve problems, including frequency tables, bar graphs, picture graphs, and line plots.	132, 136, 139, 142

Grade 5

Focal Points		Page Numbers
Number and Operations and Algebra: Division of Whole Numbers	Estimate and calculate quotients involving multidigit dividends. Apply knowledge of models, place value (to the millions), properties, multiplication, and the order of operations. Develop fluency and understanding of procedures for computation and problem solving, choosing the most appropriate form of the quotient and interpreting the remainder.	19, 25, 29, 32, 36
Number and Operations: Fractions and Decimals	Add and subtract fractions with like and unlike denominators. Relate fractions and decimals, including the use of models and place value (through millions and millionths). Estimate and calculate the sums and differences of fractions and decimals. Add and subtract to solve problems, including measurement.	63, 66, 69, 73, 77
Geometry and Measurement and Algebra: Three-Dimensional Shapes	Identify, classify, and analyze polyhedral solids by their properties (edges, faces, vertices). Identify and measure volume and surface area of three-dimensional shapes. Select appropriate units, strategies, and tools for solving problems involving estimating or measuring volume and surface area, including decomposition and using formulas.	103, 107, 110, 115
Data Analysis and Algebra	Construct and analyze data, including double-bar graphs, line graphs, and coordinate grids. Use patterns, models, graphs, number relationships, and the order of operations to write and solve simple algebraic equations and inequalities.	146, 149, 158, 163, 167

CONNECTIONS TO STANDARDS

This chart shows the National Council of Teachers of Mathematics (2005) standards covered in this book.

Grade 4

Content Standards		Page Numbers
Number and Operations	Understand numbers, ways of representing numbers, relationships among numbers, and number systems. Understand meanings of operations and how they relate to one another. Compute fluently and make reasonable estimates.	2, 6, 9, 13, 16, 42, 47, 51, 57, 61, 82, 118, 121, 124, 127
Algebra	Understand patterns, relations, and functions. Represent and analyze mathematical situations and structures using algebraic symbols. Use mathematical models to represent and understand quantitative relationships.	13, 42, 51, 87, 91, 118, 121, 124, 127

(Continued)

Content Standards		Page Numbers
Geometry	Analyze characteristics and properties of two- and three-dimensional geometric shapes, and develop mathematical arguments about geometric relationships. Specify locations and describe spatial relationships using coordinate geometry and other representational systems. Apply transformations and use symmetry to analyze mathematical situations. Use visualization, spatial reasoning, and geometric modeling to solve problems.	47, 51, 82, 87, 91, 95, 99, 142
Measurement	Understand measurable attributes of objects and the units, systems, and processes of measurement. Apply appropriate techniques, tools, and formulas to determine measurements.	82, 87, 99
Data Analysis and Probability	Formulate questions that can be addressed with data, and collect, organize, and display relevant data to answer them. Select and use appropriate statistical methods to analyze data. Develop and evaluate inferences and predictions that are based on data.	132, 136, 139
Problem Solving	Build new mathematical knowledge through problem solving. Solve problems that arise in mathematics and in other contexts. Apply and adapt a variety of appropriate strategies to solve problems. Monitor and reflect on the process of mathematical problem solving.	2, 9, 13, 16, 42, 47, 51, 57, 61, 87, 91, 95, 99, 118, 121, 124, 127, 132, 136, 139, 142
Communication	Communicate mathematical thinking coherently and clearly to peers, teachers, and others. Analyze and evaluate the mathematical thinking and strategies of others. Use the language of mathematics to express mathematical ideas precisely.	47, 51, 57, 61, 87, 91, 95, 99, 121, 124, 127, 132, 136, 139, 142
Connections	Recognize and use connections among mathematical ideas. Recognize and apply mathematics in contexts outside of mathematics.	51, 61, 99, 127
Representation	Create and use representations to organize, record, and communicate mathematical ideas. Select, apply, and translate among mathematical representations to solve problems. Use representations to model and interpret physical, social, and mathematical phenomena.	42, 47, 51, 61, 82, 87, 91, 95, 99, 127, 132, 136, 139, 142

Grade 5

Content Standards		Page Numbers
Number and Operations	Understand numbers, ways of representing numbers, relationships among numbers, and number systems. Understand meanings of operations and how they relate to one another. Compute fluently and make reasonable estimates.	19, 25, 29, 32, 36, 63, 66, 69, 73, 77, 107, 110, 115, 146, 149, 158, 163, 167

Content Standards		Page Numbers
Algebra	Understand patterns, relations, and functions. Represent and analyze mathematical situations and structures using algebraic symbols. Use mathematical models to represent and understand quantitative relationships.	19, 63, 73, 77, 107, 110, 115, 146, 158, 167
Geometry	Analyze characteristics and properties of two- and three-dimensional geometric shapes, and develop mathematical arguments about geometric relationships. Specify locations and describe spatial relationships using coordinate geometry and other representational systems. Apply transformations and use symmetry to analyze mathematical situations. Use visualization, spatial reasoning, and geometric modeling to solve problems.	63, 77, 103, 107, 115, 146, 158, 163
Measurement	Understand measurable attributes of objects and the units, systems, and processes of measurement. Apply appropriate techniques, tools, and formulas to determine measurements.	32, 73, 77, 107, 110, 115, 158, 167
Data Analysis and Probability	Formulate questions that can be addressed with data, and collect, organize, and display relevant data to answer them. Select and use appropriate statistical methods to analyze data. Develop and evaluate inferences and predictions that are based on data.	32, 73, 77, 107, 115, 146, 149, 158, 163, 167
Problem Solving	Build new mathematical knowledge through problem solving. Solve problems that arise in mathematics and in other contexts. Apply and adapt a variety of appropriate strategies to solve problems. Monitor and reflect on the process of mathematical problem solving.	19, 25, 32, 63, 69, 73, 77, 107, 110, 115, 149, 158, 167
Communication	Communicate mathematical thinking coherently and clearly to peers, teachers, and others. Analyze and evaluate the mathematical thinking and strategies of others. Use the language of mathematics to express mathematical ideas precisely.	25, 29, 32, 36, 63, 66, 69, 73, 77, 103, 107, 110, 115, 146, 149, 158, 163, 167
Connections	Recognize and use connections among mathematical ideas. Recognize and apply mathematics in contexts outside of mathematics.	32, 63, 66, 69, 73, 77, 103, 107, 110, 115, 146, 149, 158, 163, 167
Representation	Create and use representations to organize, record, and communicate mathematical ideas. Select, apply, and translate among mathematical representations to solve problems. Use representations to model and interpret physical, social, and mathematical phenomena.	19, 25, 36, 63, 66, 69, 73, 77, 103, 107, 110, 115, 146, 149, 158, 163, 167

About the Author

David A. Sousa, EdD, is an international consultant in educational neuroscience and the author of seven best-selling books on how to translate brain research into educational practice. For more than 20 years he has presented at national conventions of educational organizations and has conducted workshops on brain research and science education in hundreds of school districts and at colleges and universities across the United States, Canada, Europe, Asia, Australia, and New Zealand.

Dr. Sousa has a bachelor of science degree in chemistry from Massachusetts State College at Bridgewater, a master of arts in teaching degree in science from Harvard University, and a doctorate from Rutgers University. He has taught high school science, has served as a K–12 director of science, and was superintendent of the New Providence, New Jersey, public schools. He has been an adjunct professor of education at Seton Hall University and a visiting lecturer at Rutgers University. He is a past president of the National Staff Development Council.

Dr. Sousa has also edited science books and published articles in leading educational journals. He has received awards from professional associations and school districts for his commitment and contributions to research, staff development, and science education. He is a member of the Cognitive Neuroscience Society, and he has appeared on the NBC *Today* show and on National Public Radio to discuss his work with schools using brain research.

1

Multiplication and Division

THE MYSTERY OF THE MIXED-UP PARTY LISTS

Objective

Students will work in groups to find the least common multiple.

Anticipatory Set

Speaking with the excited tone of a news reporter, announce to students, "Eight girls and boys were each planning their own birthday party. Each person was carrying a party list with the number of guests. They were all shopping at the same store to buy party supplies when suddenly the lights went out! Somehow, their party lists got mixed up. They don't remember how many guests are invited or how many supplies to buy. It is your job to help solve the mystery!"

Purpose

Tell students that they are detectives needed to solve a mystery. Their job is to use clues to figure out the number of guests each boy or girl invited to his or her party and exactly how many of each item to buy.

Input

Tell students that they will be working with multiples as clues: "A *multiple* of a number is the product of that number and another whole number." On the board, write two tables with examples of multiples. Across the top row of each table, write the numbers *1* through *12*. Across the bottom row of the first table, write multiples of 3 up to 36. Across the bottom row of the second table, write multiples of 5 up to 60.

Explain that the *least common multiple* is the smallest number into which two numbers can both be evenly divided. One way to find the least common multiple of two numbers is to make two tables. One table lists the multiples of one number. The other table lists the multiples of the other number. Compare the two tables with students, and circle the smallest number that appears on both lists. Explain that 15 is the least common multiple for the numbers *3* and *5*.

Modeling

Divide the class into eight small groups. Place a transparency of a multiplication table on the overhead projector, and give each student a photocopy. Review the table so students understand how to use it.

Provide an example so students can create their own tables. Say, "Pretend we are going to the store to buy prizes for a party. Toy cars come in packages of four. Balloons come in packages of seven. We want to buy the same number of toy cars and balloons. To help us find this number, we can draw two tables of multiples."

Distribute ½-in (1.27 cm) graph paper to students. On the board, draw two tables with two rows each. Have students copy the tables onto their graph paper. Across the top of one table, write the numbers *1* through *12*. Label this row "Packages of Toy Cars." Across the bottom row, ask volunteers to suggest multiples of 4 for you to write. Encourage students to refer to their multiplication table as a guide. Label this row "Total # of Cars."

Draw a similar table for the packages of balloons, using multiples of 7. Have students copy the second table onto their graph paper. After both tables are completed, ask students to circle the smallest number in both tables. Ask, "What is the least number of packages of toy cars we need to buy?" (*7*), "What is the least number of packages of balloons we need to buy?" (*4*), and "What is the least common multiple of 7 and 4?" (*28*).

The Mystery of the Mixed-Up Party Lists												
Packages of Toy Cars	1	2	3	4	5	6	7	8	9	10	11	12
Total # of Cars	4	8	12	16	20	24	28	32	36	40	44	48

Packages of Balloons	1	2	3	4	5	6	7	8	9	10	11	12
Total # of Balloons	7	14	21	28	35	42	49	56	63	70	77	84

Checking for Understanding

Check to make sure students know how to draw tables comparing two multiples. Remind them that the least common multiple is the smallest number in both tables.

Guided Practice

Give each group a party gift bag. Each bag should contain one of eight cards cut from the **Shopping List Cards reproducibles (pages 4–5).** Inform groups that the clues they need to solve the mystery are in the gift bags. Instruct them to read the clues and make two tables of multiples on their graph paper. Students will use the information from these tables to answer the questions and solve the mystery of the mixed-up party lists.

Closure

Afterward, ask each group to read aloud its clues, report its answers, and explain how its members reached their conclusions. Then ask students to reflect on what they learned in their math journals.

Independent Practice

Place the gift bags at a math center with multiplication tables, graph paper, and pencils. Invite students to visit the center and solve the mystery of the mixed-up party lists following the clues in other groups' gift bags. Number each gift bag, and provide a self-check by writing the answers to each card on the bottom of the corresponding bag.

Shopping List Cards 1–4

1. Chad is buying prizes for his birthday party. Toy racecars are sold in packages of 9. Rubber snakes are sold in packages of 4. To have the same number of cars and snakes:

   a. What is the least number of packages of cars he needs to buy?

   b. What is the least number of packages of snakes he needs to buy?

   c. What is the least common multiple of 9 and 4?

   d. If the number of Chad's guests is the same as the least common multiple of 9 and 4, how many guests did he invite?

2. Jake is buying candy for his birthday party. Candy bars are sold in packages of 8. Peppermints are sold in packages of 5. To have the same number of candy bars and peppermints:

   a. What is the least number of packages of candy bars he needs to buy?

   b. What is the least number of packages of peppermints he needs to buy?

   c. What is the least common multiple of 8 and 5?

   d. If the number of Jake's guests is the same as the least common multiple of 8 and 5, how many guests did he invite?

3. Megan is buying party supplies for her birthday party. Paper plates are sold in packages of 5. Paper napkins are sold in packages of 6. To have the same number of plates and napkins:

   a. What is the least number of packages of paper plates she needs to buy?

   b. What is the least number of packages of paper napkins she needs to buy?

   c. What is the least common multiple of 5 and 6?

   d. If the number of Megan's guests is the same as the least common multiple of 5 and 6, how many guests did she invite?

4. Katrina is buying hot dogs and hot dog buns to serve at her birthday party. Hot dogs are sold in packages of 6. Hot dog buns are sold in packages of 8. To have the same number of hot dogs and hot dog buns:

   a. What is the least number of packages of hot dogs she needs to buy?

   b. What is the least number of packages of hot dog buns she needs to buy?

   c. What is the least common multiple of 6 and 8?

   d. If the number of Katrina's guests is the same as the least common multiple of 6 and 8, how many guests did she invite?

Shopping List Cards 5–8

5. Isabel is buying party supplies for her birthday party. Plastic spoons are sold in packages of 9. Plastic forks are sold in packages of 8. To have the same number of spoons and forks:

   a. What is the least number of packages of spoons she needs to buy?
   b. What is the least number of packages of forks she needs to buy?
   c. What is the least common multiple of 9 and 8?
   d. If the number of Isabel's guests is the same as the least common multiple of 9 and 8, how many guests did she invite?

6. Shakir is buying small bags of chips and pretzels to serve at his birthday party. Bags of chips are sold in packages of 4. Bags of pretzels are sold in packages of 5. To have the same number of bags of chips and pretzels:

   a. What is the least number of packages of chip bags he needs to buy?
   b. What is the least number of packages of pretzel bags he needs to buy?
   c. What is the least common multiple of 4 and 5?
   d. If the number of Shakir's guests is the same as the least common multiple of 4 and 5, how many guests did he invite?

7. Hannah is buying prizes to give away at her birthday party. Bracelets are sold in packages of 6. Hair clips are sold in packages of 3. To have the same number of bracelets and hair clips:

   a. What is the least number of packages of bracelets she needs to buy?
   b. What is the least number of packages of hair clips she needs to buy?
   c. What is the least common multiple of 6 and 3?
   d. If the number of Hannah's guests is the same as the least common multiple of 6 and 3, how many guests did she invite?

8. Jamal is buying party supplies for his birthday party. Glow string is sold in packages of 7. Noisemakers are sold in packages of 9. To have the same number of cans of glow string and noisemakers:

   a. What is the least number of packages of glow string he needs to buy?
   b. What is the least number of packages of noisemakers he needs to buy?
   c. What is the least common multiple of 7 and 9?
   d. If the number of Jamal's guests is the same as the least common multiple of 7 and 9, how many guests did he invite?

MEET THE FACT FAMILY

Objective

Students will work in groups to identify fact families for sets of numbers.

> By simply adding a visual representation of a situation that is relevant to students, greater meaning can be obtained.

Anticipatory Set

Draw two rows of three triangles on the board. Ask volunteers to state a multiplication equation that describes the triangle arrangement ($2 \times 3 = 6$ or $3 \times 2 = 6$). Write both equations on the board. Repeat the activity, and ask students to state a division equation that describes the triangles ($6 \div 2 = 3$ or $6 \div 3 = 2$). Write both equations on the board.

Purpose

Ask for a volunteer who has four family members. Make a chart on the board. Write that student's last name at the top of the chart. Underneath, list the four family members' names.

Make a second chart on the board. At the top of the chart, write the numbers *2, 3,* and *6*. Explain to students that just as each of them has a family, each set of numbers has a family called a *fact family*. Say, "A fact family shows the multiplication and division equations that can be written for a set of numbers." On the chart, list the four equations for the fact family *2, 3,* and *6*.

The Lee Family
Mr. Lee
Mrs. Lee
Eric
Mina

The Fact Family for *2, 3,* and *6*
$2 \times 3 = 6$
$3 \times 2 = 6$
$6 \div 2 = 3$
$6 \div 3 = 2$

Input

Tell students, "Learning fact families will help you to multiply and divide. Just as identifying people in a family helps us see how they are related, identifying the fact family for a set of numbers helps us see how multiplication and division facts are related."

Write a set of numbers on the board, such as *3, 5,* and *15*. Say, "This is a set of numbers." Write the fact family for this number set on the board: $3 \times 5 = 15$, $5 \times 3 = 15$, $15 \div 3 = 5$, $15 \div 5 = 3$. Explain, "These multiplication and division equations form the fact family for this set of numbers." Ask volunteers to share how knowing a multiplication equation in a fact family, such as $3 \times 5 = 15$, can help them to answer a division problem such as $15 \div 3$.

Modeling

In this activity, students will work in small groups to write multiplication and division equations that form a fact family for an assigned set of numbers. They will then present these equations in a mock TV game show.

Model how to find the fact family for the number set *4, 3,* and *12.* Write the number set on the board. Say, "To identify the fact family for this set of numbers, first think of multiplication equations using these numbers. Write these equations on a piece of paper. The equations are $4 \times 3 = 12$ and $3 \times 4 = 12$. Now think of division equations using these numbers. Write these equations on a piece of paper. The equations are $12 \div 4 = 3$ and $12 \div 3 = 4$."

Model other examples on the board.

Checking for Understanding

Ask students to confirm that they understand the meaning of *fact family* and how to find the fact family for a set of numbers. If students need further instruction, provide more models on the board.

Guided Practice

Divide the class into groups of four. If you have two extra students, form them into a group, and be sure to give them a set of numbers that has only two equations in its fact family, such as *3, 3,* and *9.* (If you have only one student remaining, he or she can join a group to practice finding the fact family and then act as the announcer for the TV show.)

Give each student a small index card and scrap paper. Distribute to each group one large index card on which you have written one set of numbers, such as *9, 7, 63; 8, 5, 40; 7, 3, 21; 6, 7, 42; 5, 9, 45; 4, 6, 24; 3, 8, 24;* or *2, 5, 10.* Be sure each large index card has a unique set of numbers. Instruct students to work together in their groups to think of the multiplication and division equations that form the fact family for their group's number set. Encourage them to write their answers on scrap paper first.

Then have each student in the group choose one of the four equations to write on his or her own small index card. Each student should choose a different equation. When groups are finished, check to make sure each student has written a different equation for the group's number set.

Explain that students will now participate in a mock TV game show called Meet the Fact Family. Ask a student announcer to invite one group of students to stand while he or she announces, "Meet the fact family for the number set [X, Y, Z]!" (The announcer should state the number set written on the large index card for that group.) Ask all four students in the group to stand and take turns announcing their "names" by stating the equations on their small index cards. Encourage the class to applaud after the family is introduced. Ask group members to place their small index cards in a basket to use for the upcoming game.

Introduce each group the same way until all small index cards are collected in a basket. Mix up the cards in the basket, and then allow each student to choose a card at random. Instruct students to place their cards facedown on their desks and wait for the signal to start the game. When the announcer says "Go," have students turn over the cards. The goal of the game is for each student to find the other members of his or her new fact family before time is up. When they find all the members of their fact families, they should stand together and "freeze" in place. After about 1 minute, the announcer should say, "Freeze!" Every group that has found its entire fact family within that time is a winner.

Closure

Invite volunteers to draw sets of triangles arranged in rows on the board. (Be sure that within each arrangement, there is the same number of triangles in each row.) Ask students to think of and share an equation that describes each arrangement.

Independent Practice

At the math center, place a small basket of index cards that each have a set of numbers listed on one side and the corresponding fact family written on the other. Provide paper, pencils, and a jar of manipulatives, such as dried macaroni. Encourage students to visit the math center and choose an index card from the basket. They should place the index card faceup on the table to show the number set and then arrange the manipulatives in equal rows to represent that set. Tell them to write the multiplication and division equations for the number set and then self-check their work by turning over the index card to see the fact family on the back.

Then have students write in their math journals in response to the question, "How does knowing the fact family for a set of numbers help me with math?"

GUESS-TIMATE ESTIMATES

Objective

Students will imagine real-life situations to estimate products.

Anticipatory Set

Ask students, "If 687 students are expected to buy school lunches this year, about how many school lunches does the cafeteria need to prepare each week?" Challenge students to think about a logical way to find the answer. Ask them if it is possible to find the exact answer (*No. Some days, students might be absent, and they would need fewer lunches. Other days, the cafeteria might serve pizza, and more students would buy lunches.*). Say, "Sometimes it is not necessary or possible to find an exact answer to a math problem. For some math problems, estimating an answer helps provide a reasonable guess for the solution."

> Students need to recognize that many things cannot and need not be measured precisely.

Purpose

Tell students that estimating can help provide reasonable answers for problems that cannot or do not need to be measured in exact quantities. For this activity, they will practice determining the number of plates of food served by different restaurants.

Input

Review how to round numbers to their greatest place value. Write a number between 100 and 10,000 on the board. Say, "Let's round this number to the nearest hundred." Have each student whisper his or her answer to the classmate sitting next to him or her. Invite a volunteer to share the answer. Repeat the activity with several more numbers.

Write a number between 1,000 and 10,000 on the board. Say, "Let's round this number to the nearest thousand." Have each student whisper his or her answer to the classmate sitting next to him or her. Again, invite a volunteer to share the answer. Repeat the activity using several more numbers. Explain, "When we estimate, first round the number to its greatest place value."

Then repeat the original question: "If 687 students are expected to buy school lunches this year, about how many school lunches does the cafeteria need to prepare each week?" Remind students that a school week has 5 days. Ask a volunteer to explain a logical way to find the answer (*Round the number to 700, and multiply by 5.*). Ask, "Why is 3,500 a reasonable answer to this problem?"

Modeling

Tell students they will play a game to practice estimating products. First, you will give them a multiplication problem. Then, they will round the larger number. Finally, they will multiply this new set of numbers and write the answer.

Divide the class into four teams. Invite one player from each team to stand at the board. Instruct each of the four players to write "493 × 5" on the board. When you say, "Go," have them round the larger number to 500, multiply it by the smaller number, and then write the answer. The first team to write the correct answer scores one point. Continue playing the game using new team members and new problems for each round until every student has had a turn at the board.

Checking for Understanding

Check to make sure everyone understands how to round numbers. Ask a volunteer to explain the steps to estimate a product. Remind students that for this activity, they are rounding only the larger number. The smaller number remains the same.

Guided Practice

Copy the **What's on the Menu? reproducible (page 11)** onto a transparency, and distribute copies to students. Read the sentences on the plate together, and complete a sample as a class. Instruct students to follow the instructions on the plate to complete their reproducibles. Have them cut out their plates and glue them to construction paper and then decorate the paper with crayons or markers to resemble a place setting. When finished, have students write the answers to their problems on the back.

Ask students to exchange papers with partners and solve their partners' problems. Students can check their answers on the back. Invite them to continue trading place settings with different classmates as time allows.

Closure

Remind students that some things cannot or do not require an exact answer. When estimating, they should round numbers to their greatest place value. Have students answer the following questions in their math journals: "How can estimating help you plan a birthday party, a school carnival, or a soccer league pizza party? When multiplying two numbers, how can estimating help you check if your answer is reasonable?"

Independent Practice

For homework, have students complete a copy of the **Guess-timate Estimates reproducible (page 12).** Review how to round numbers to their greatest place value.

What's on the Menu?

Directions: Fill out the paper plate. Then cut it out and glue it to a piece of construction paper. Draw a napkin, knife, fork, spoon, and cup on the construction paper to make a place setting as shown.

_____'s Restaurant
(person's name)

serves _____.
(name of food)

It's everyone's favorite choice on the menu!

The restaurant serves _____ plates of it every day.
(number between 100 and 10,000)

If the restaurant is open

_____ days a week,
(number between 1 and 7)

about how many plates does it serve each week?

Name_____ Date_____

Guess-timate Estimates

Directions: Estimate each product by rounding the greater number.

1. 84
   × 6
   _____
   Estimate: _____

2. 7,968
   ×   3
   _____
   Estimate: _____

3. 987
   ×   5
   _____
   Estimate: _____

4. 2,103
   ×   7
   _____
   Estimate: _____

5. 52
   × 4
   _____
   Estimate: _____

6. 378
   ×   9
   _____
   Estimate: _____

7. 8,014
   ×   2
   _____
   Estimate: _____

8. 27
   × 8
   _____
   Estimate: _____

9. 122
   ×   5
   _____
   Estimate: _____

10. 493
    ×   3
    _____
    Estimate: _____

Directions: Write a number between 100 and 10,000 on each line. Then estimate the product.

11. _____ × 4 = _____

12. _____ × 7 = _____

POINT AND PLAY

Objective

Students will use quick recall of multiplication facts and recognize patterns of zero to play a call-and-response game.

Anticipatory Set

Write four progressive multiplication problems on the board, each one below the one before it: "3×4, 30×4, 30×40, 300×40." Invite students to compare and contrast the examples. Ask, "How are these equations the same? How are they different? Do you recognize any patterns?" Guide the discussion until students are able to identify that each example has the same basic multiplication fact (3×4) but that different numbers of zeros are in the factors.

Purpose

Explain that when one is working with math and numbers, it helps to look for patterns: "When multiplying multiples of 10 and 100, you can first identify the basic multiplication fact and then count the number of zeros to find the answer."

> The brain's ability to detect patterns and make associations is one of its greatest strengths.

Input

Inform students that when multiplying multiples of 10 and 100, they should ask three questions: What is the fact? How many zeros? What is the answer? Write these questions on the board next to the four equations. Use an edible pointer such as a pretzel rod or a powdered candy straw. Point to and ask each question aloud, encouraging students to read along with you: "What is the fact? How many zeros? What is the answer?"

Modeling

Use the pointer to point to the equation 3×4. Then point to the first question, and say it aloud in unison: "What is the fact?" Write the answer on the board: "$3 \times 4 = 12$." Point to the second question, and say it aloud in unison: "How many zeros?" Write the answer: "0." Point to the third question, and say it aloud in unison: "What is the answer?" Write the answer: "12." Repeat the process using the equation 30×4: "What is the fact?" ($3 \times 4 = 12$); "How many zeros?" (1); and "What is the answer?" (120).

Explain that the class is going to play a call-and-response game to practice multiplying multiples of 10 and 100. Divide the class into two teams. Have the teams move their desks so they are facing each other. Give an edible pointer to a player on Team 1.

Begin the game by pointing to the third equation on the board: 30×40. Have Team 1 ask the first question in unison: "What is the fact?" The pointer (player with the edible pointer) points to a player on Team 2 to give the answer

($3 \times 4 = 12$). Team 1 then asks the second question in unison: "How many zeros?" The pointer points to a different player on Team 2 to give the answer (2). Finally, Team 1 asks the third question in unison: "What is the answer?" The pointer then points to a third player on Team 2 to give the answer (1,200). Invite this student to write the answer on the board.

Ask teams to repeat this process using the remaining equation. This time, give a pointer to a player on Team 2. Team 2 will now call out the questions and point to players on Team 1 to respond with answers.

Checking for Understanding

Check to make sure everyone understands how to play the game. Invite a volunteer to explain the steps to multiply multiples of 10 and 100. Model more examples as needed.

Guided Practice

Invite the teams to continue playing the game, making sure each player gets a chance to be the pointer. Give each player a fresh edible pointer to use. For the game, write four sets of similar equations on the board, such as 7×2, 70×2, 70×20, 700×20 and 5×3, 50×3, 50×30, 500×30. As students become more familiar with the process, refer to the **Multiplying Multiples reproducible (page 15)** for more examples to use during the game.

Closure

After every player has a turn as the pointer, award the class by letting them eat their edible pointers. Ask students to write in their math journals about the highlights of playing the game. Instruct them to answer the following question: "How did looking for and identifying patterns help you find the answers?"

Independent Practice

Reinforce the concept of how to multiply multiples of 10 and 100 by having students complete the Multiplying Multiples reproducible. Instruct them to fill in each answer with one digit per box.

Extending the Activity

Read aloud the book *How Much Is a Million?* by David M. Schwartz. Then play an exciting game of Point and Play using multiples of 100 and 1,000 such as $30,000 \times 8,000$. Help students identify each large number by its correct name. Each time a product equals 1 million or greater, celebrate by having students congratulate themselves with cheers or high fives.

Name_____   Date_____

Multiplying Multiples

Directions: Find each product. Write the answers in the crossword puzzle, one digit per box.

Down

1. 70 × 600
2. 400 × 90
3. 90 × 300
4. 30 × 50
7. 800 × 80
9. 90 × 90
11. 3 × 30
13. 6 × 90
14. 400 × 6
16. 3 × 80

Across

5. 80 × 900
6. 80 × 700
7. 20 × 3
8. 700 × 40
10. 2 × 20
12. 900 × 50
14. 300 × 7
15. 200 × 60
17. 20 × 70
18. 600 × 30

200 CATCH GAME

Objective

Students will play a game and keep score using positive and negative numbers.

Anticipatory Set

Using the **200 Catch Game reproducible (page 18)** as a guide, draw a large vertical number line on the board or a long sheet of butcher paper taped to a classroom wall. Label the number line in increments of 25, starting with −200 at the bottom and ending with 200 at the top. For the 0 mark, draw a horizontal line at least 12 in across.

Point out the number line to students. Ask them to imagine a vertical number line outside where the ground represents 0. Draw grass and flowers on the 0 line to help students visualize this picture. Point to the positive integers on the number line. Explain that these numbers are above ground. Draw a sun and clouds at the top of the number line. Point to the negative integers. These numbers go down into a hole in the ground.

Purpose

Next to the number line, write the following scores: "Fly ball = 100 points, 1 bounce = 75 points, 2 bounces = 50 points, 3 or more bounces = 25 points." Explain that the class will be playing an outdoor ball game to earn these points. For instance, if students catch a fly ball, it is plus 100 points. If they try to catch the ball but drop it, it is minus 100 points. If the ball bounces once and they catch it, it is plus 75 points. Students will mentally add and subtract numbers up and down the number line to keep their own score.

Input

Inform students that numbers "above ground" are called *positive numbers.* (Point to the top half of the number line.) Positive numbers are all greater than 0. There is also a group of numbers called *negative numbers.* These numbers are less than 0. (Point to the bottom half of the number line that is "below ground.")

Ask students to identify the difference between positive and negative numbers on the number line (*Negative numbers have a minus sign in front of them.*). Invite students to look for a pattern on the number line (*Negative numbers continue in the same order as positive numbers except in the opposite direction from 0.*).

Modeling

For this game, divide the class into small teams. Explain that one player hits a tennis ball using a racquetball racquet while the other players try to catch the ball. Players earn points based on whether the hit results in a fly ball or bounces once, twice, or three or more times before they capture the ball.

When a player catches the ball, he or she earns a positive number of points. When a player drops the ball, he or she earns a negative number of points. Players will mentally keep track of their own points while they play, and a scorekeeper will keep track on paper. The first player to score 200 points is next up "at bat."

Model how to play the game in the classroom. Invite one student to the front of the room. Gently toss him or her a tennis ball. If the student catches a fly ball, ask the score (*100 points*). If the student drops the ball, ask the score (*–100 points*). Point to that number on the number line. Then toss the tennis ball to the student so it bounces one time, two times, and three times. Ask the score each time, and point to those numbers on the number line.

Checking for Understanding

Take time for students to confirm that they understand how to keep score for the game. Ask volunteers to take turns catching the tennis ball, stating each new score aloud.

Guided Practice

Move to an outdoor playing field. Divide the class into teams of 6 to 10 players. Be sure to distribute players who have prior baseball or softball experience among the teams. Provide each team with one tennis ball, one racquetball racquet, a clipboard, paper, and a pencil for scorekeeping. One player on each team is the scorekeeper, one is the "batter," and the rest are in the outfield. Position each team on the field or playground so it does not interfere with other teams as they play.

Have students watch as one team demonstrates how to play the game. The batter hits the ball out to the field. The last person to catch or touch the ball before dropping it scores points for that hit. Have each player mentally compute and then state his or her score aloud before tossing the ball back to the batter.

Invite teams to play simultaneously. Switch batters when someone scores 200 points, or have the player with the highest score become the new batter after about 5 minutes of play. The last batter becomes the new scorekeeper, and the scorekeeper joins the outfield. Each new game begins with everyone's score at 0. Continue to play for 15 to 20 minutes, instructing teams to switch batters about every 5 minutes.

Closure

When you return to the classroom, ask volunteers to share their highest and lowest scores. Prompt students to write in their math journals about their game experiences. Ask them to draw number lines in their journals and mark their highest and lowest scores.

Independent Practice

Have each student complete a copy of the 200 Catch Game reproducible for homework. Remind students that negative numbers continue in the same order as positive numbers, except in the opposite direction from 0.

Name_____   Date_____

200 Catch Game

Directions: Use the number line to help you find the answers.

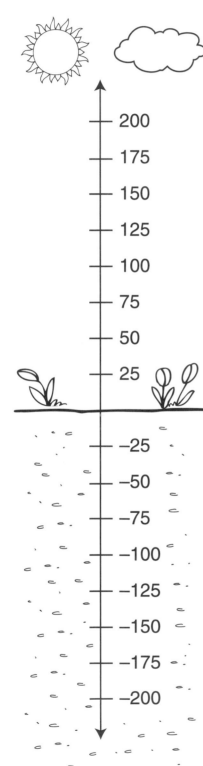

1. Felipe scored 100 points and then 50 points. What was his final score? _____

2. Sara scored −25 points, then 75 points, then 50 points. What was her final score? _____

3. Carlos scored 75 points, then −25 points, then 100 points, then 25 points. What was his final score? _____

4. Ryan scored 25 points, then −100 points, then −50 points. What was his final score? _____

5. Kelli scored −50 points, then −100 points, then −50 points. What was her final score? _____

6. Carmen scored −75 points and then 100 points. What was her final score? _____

7. Luke scored −75 points and then 50 points. What was his final score? _____

8 Jackson scored −100 points, then 100 points, then −50 points. What was his final score? _____

9. Emma scored 25 points, then 25 points, then 75 points. What was her final score? _____

10. Alex scored 50 points, then −75 points, then 100 points. What was his final score? _____

11. Lisette scored 100 points, then 25 points, then 75 points. What was her final score? _____

12. Jenny scored −25 points, then 25 points, then 50 points. What was her final score? _____

13. Who had the lowest score? _____

14. Who had the highest score? _____

BLOCKS OF DIVISION

Objective

Students will use place-value blocks and pictures to solve long division.

Anticipatory Set

Write the following situation on the board, and give students a few moments to think about the answer before asking them to respond:

"Gumballs are sold in bags, in tubes, and individually. Each bag holds 100 gumballs, and each tube holds 10 gumballs. If three children are given a total of 3 bags, 4 tubes, and 2 individual gumballs to share equally, how can we figure out how many gumballs each child gets?" (*divide*).

Purpose

Remind students that *division* is the process by which a starting number, or amount, is divided or distributed into equal groups. Then tell them that they will use place-value blocks and pictures to show what it actually means to divide a large number into equal groups through *long division* before they write and solve it numerically.

Input

Display a set of place-value blocks, and remind students that each square flat represents 100, each stick represents 10, and each small cube represents 1. Stack the blocks to show the equivalent amounts (1 flat = 10 sticks; 1 stick = 10 cubes).

On the board, draw simple picture representations of the place-value blocks, drawing a large square for the hundreds flat, a vertical line for the tens stick, and a dot for the ones cube. Label the pictures "1 hundred (100)," "1 ten (10)," and "1 one (1)."

Explain to students that they can use place-value blocks and pictures to help them solve a division problem, such as the gumball example, showing how to distribute and regroup amounts as they solve each step of the division process.

> Arithmetic and mathematical knowledge should be based first on concrete situations rather than abstract concepts. Numerical representations help students develop mental models of arithmetic that connect to their intuitive number sense.

Modeling

Return to the gumball example, and remind students that each bag contains 100, just like the hundreds flat, and each tube contains 10, just like the tens stick. Then write the following on the board, using place-value blocks to model the 3 bags (flats), 4 tubes (sticks), and 2 individual gumballs (cubes):

$$3 \text{ bags, 4 tubes, 2 individual gumballs} =$$
$$3 \text{ hundreds, 4 tens, 2 ones} =$$
$$300 + 40 + 2 =$$
$$342$$

Remind students that there are three children sharing the gumballs equally, which means dividing the amount into three equal groups (one group per child). Write

> 342 gumballs divided into 3 equal groups
>
> $342 \div 3 = ?$
>
> $3\overline{)342}$

Draw a picture model of the division setup, showing a row of three squares, four vertical lines, and two dots (flats, sticks, cubes) inside a division bracket for the dividend *342*. Draw three stick people in front of the bracket to represent the divisor *3*.

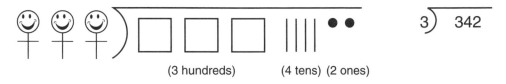

(3 hundreds)   (4 tens) (2 ones)

Then use three volunteers to help model each step of the division process, starting with the greatest place value, the hundreds. Ask students the following questions:

- How many flats does each child get? (*1*). Give each volunteer one flat.
- How many gumballs does each child have so far? (*100 gumballs*).
- Are there any flats leftover? (*no*).

Draw the first step on the board. Write the numeric calculations next to the picture.

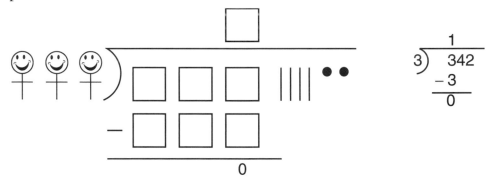

Continue with the next place value, the tens. Ask students the following:

- How many sticks does each child get? (*1*). Give each volunteer one stick.
- How many gumballs does each child have so far? (*100 + 10 = 110 gumballs*).
- Are there any sticks leftover? (*yes*).

Point out that there is one stick leftover since there is not enough for each child to have two sticks. To continue the division, the leftover stick must be traded for smaller pieces that can be shared equally. Show how to exchange one stick for 10 ones cubes. Ask students, "If we trade one stick for 10 cubes (an equivalent amount), how many ones do we have now?" (*2 originally + 10 more = 12 ones*). Show your computation on the board, both pictorially and numerically.

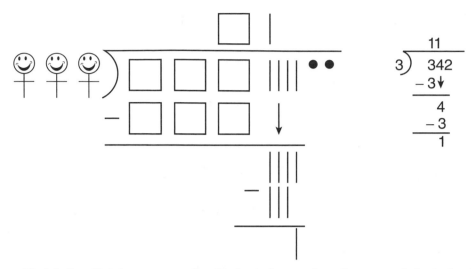

Finish the division process for the last place value, the ones. Ask students the following:

- How many cubes does each child get? (*4*). Give each volunteer four cubes.
- How many gumballs does each child have now? (*100 + 10 + 4 = 114 gumballs*).
- Are there any cubes leftover? (*no*).

Model how to check the final answer using multiplication (inverse operation):

(114 gumballs in each group × 3 groups) + 0 remainder = 342 total

Then show how to write the answer as an equation: 342 ÷ 3 = 114.

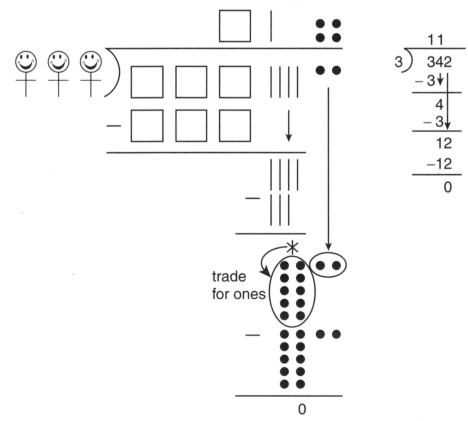

trade for ones

Checking for Understanding

Ask students to close their eyes and visualize the problem they just solved, reviewing the division process step by step. Prompt them to describe what was done first, next, and last. Then ask, "Why is it important to know how to divide?" (*Possible answer: so you can distribute equal amounts when sharing things with others*). "Why should you always divide a number from greatest to least place value (from left to right)?" (*Possible answer: so you can trade and regroup*).

Guided Practice

Give students a copy of the **Blocks of Division reproducible (page 23)**, a set of place-value blocks (or use copies of the **Place Value Grid reproducible [page 24]**), and sheets of drawing paper. Remind students that each flat represents 100, each stick represents 10, and each cube represents 1.

Read the first problem aloud as students follow along silently. Ask, "How is this problem different from our example?" (*There is one more bag of gumballs, or a total of 442 gumballs.*). Have students work with partners or in small groups to solve the problem using place-value blocks. Then show them the division process, writing the final answer as an equation: "$442 \div 3 = 147$ R1." Have students self-check and correct their work. Ask, "How did the extra bag of gumballs affect the solution? How were the steps of this division problem different from our example?"

Closure

Have students discuss and review with a partner the sequence of steps they should follow when solving long division problems. Ask them to write the steps in their math journals. Encourage them to include an example using pictures and numbers.

Independent Practice

For homework, have students finish the Blocks of Division reproducible, encouraging them to use their place-value blocks and the examples from class to help them solve each problem. Assess students' work based on completeness and accuracy of the division process, both pictorially and computationally. Invite students to share the problem they wrote and challenge classmates to solve it.

Name_____ Date_____

Blocks of Division

Directions: Solve each problem. Draw pictures of place-value blocks to show each step of the division. Then use numbers to write the same solution.

1. Gumballs are sold in bags, in tubes, and individually. Each bag has 100 gumballs, and each tube has 10 gumballs. If 3 friends get 4 bags, 4 tubes, and 2 individual gumballs to share equally, how many gumballs does each friend get?

Draw the Solution	Write the Solution

Final answer: _____ ÷ _____ = _____

2. If 5 friends get 3 bags, 7 tubes, and 5 individual gumballs to share equally, how many gumballs does each friend get?

Draw the Solution	Write the Solution

Final answer: _____ ÷ _____ = _____

Write Your Own Problem

Directions: On the back of this paper, write your own division problem with a dividend of at least three digits. Then draw and write the solution.

Place Value Grid

Directions: Copy, laminate, and cut apart this grid to make sets of 100s, 10s, and 1s for students. Store each set in a resealable plastic bag.

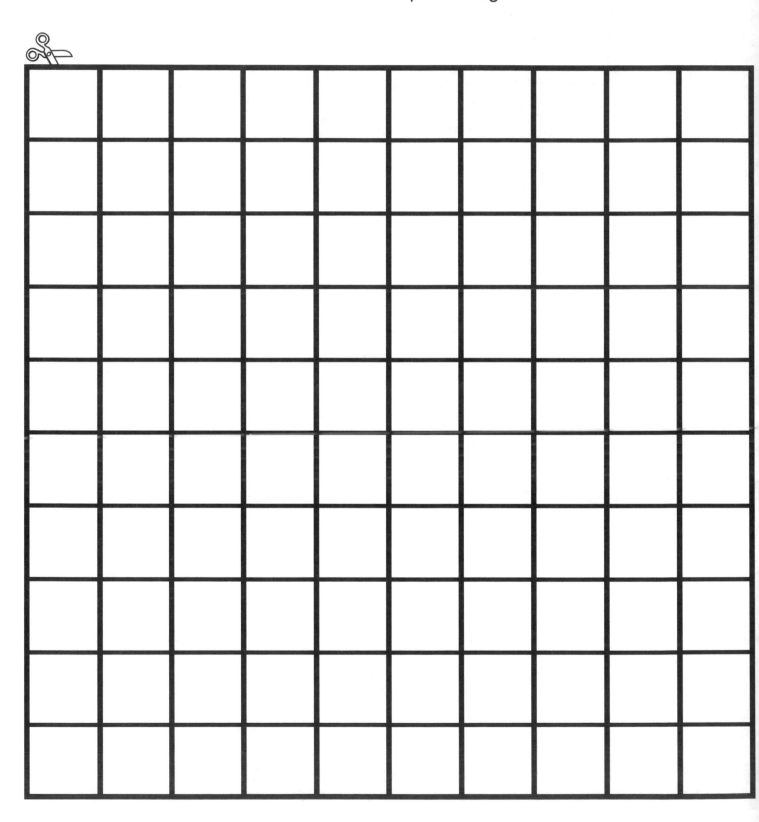

WORDS OF DIVISION

Objective

Students will complete a word chart and division puzzle using correct terminology and equations.

Anticipatory Set

Write the following prompt in a thought bubble on the board: "How many division words do you know?" Ask students to brainstorm a list of words that describe or tell about division. After 1 minute, have pairs of students compare their words.

Purpose

Tell students that using correct terminology is important when communicating math ideas and solutions. In this activity, they will use their knowledge of division terminology and equations to complete a division crossword puzzle.

Input

Give students a copy of the **Words of Division Chart reproducible (page 28)**. Display a transparency of the chart on the overhead projector. Then write the following vocabulary words on the board in random order: *dividend, divisor, divisible, quotient, remainder, compatible, inverse, regroup, operation,* and *equation.*

Read the vocabulary list aloud with students, and point out that the words are all about division. Ask students to help you decide the correct vocabulary word to write for each definition. Read aloud the first definition on the chart, and tell students to think about the correct answer. After a moment, write the answer on your chart while students copy it onto their own charts. Repeat with the remaining words.

Write an example for each vocabulary word, either a regular division equation (numbers only), an algebraic division equation (numbers and variables), or a word problem. (You might refer to problems in your math textbook.) Give students a few minutes to mentally solve each problem before you write the correct answer, for example, "The quotient of $1,035 \div 5 = $ ____" (*207*). Then have them write the example and the correct answer on their charts.

> Graphic organizers are one type of visual tool that not only get students' attention but are also valuable devices for improving understanding, meaning, and retention.

Modeling

Show students how to use their completed Words of Division Charts to help them create a division crossword puzzle:

1. Give each student a sheet of grid paper stapled to the top of white construction paper, leaving room below the grid to write the crossword clues.

2. Have students write two column titles for the clues, "Across" and "Down." (If needed, review the general setup of a crossword puzzle.)

3. Use a transparency or chart-sized grid paper to demonstrate how to write the first across clue, and outline the corresponding number of connected grid boxes in a row, one box per letter or digit. Refer to the Words of Division Chart when writing a clue for each vocabulary word.

For example, for the following clue, outline a row of eight connected grid boxes for the answer *quotient*. Write the location number in the top left corner of the first box of the answer.

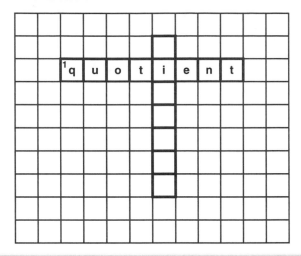

Across

1. The number *207* in the equation 1,035 ÷ 5 = 207.

4. Demonstrate how to write the first down clue, outlining the corresponding number of connected grid boxes in a downward column, one box per letter or digit. Make sure to use one of the letters or digits from the first across answer to connect the answers together.

For example, for the following clue, you may use the letter *i* (or the letter *o*) in *quotient* as part of the downward answer *divisor.*

Across

1. The number *207* in the equation
    1,035 ÷ 5 = 207.

Down

5. The number *30* in the equation
    9,000 ÷ 30 = 300.

Guided Practice

Guide students as they complete their crossword puzzles. Call on volunteers to suggest and help write clues for the remaining vocabulary words, showing how to outline those boxes on the crossword grid. Remind students that the crossword should consist of interconnecting answer boxes. After they complete their puzzles, give students a second sheet of grid paper to trace a duplicate crossword outline and fill in the correct answers to make an answer key.

Checking for Understanding

Ask a volunteer to explain how to solve and fill in the answers of a crossword puzzle. Have students demonstrate how to read a clue and fill in the correct answer on their answer keys.

Closure

Ask students to exchange crossword puzzles with classmates to solve. Ask students to summarize in their math journals what they learned in today's lesson and how it connected to something they had previously learned.

Independent Practice

For homework, have each student make a different crossword puzzle using the division terminology, including an answer key. Remind students to refer to their Words of Division Charts and to include other examples, such as division of greater numbers or multistep problems. Specify that the division problems must include dividends with at least three digits. You might also encourage them to use computer technology to help generate their crossword puzzles.

Extending the Activity

Challenge students to create a word search, a word scramble, or another creative math puzzle that includes a combination of operations ($\times, \div, +, -$).

Words of Division Chart

Directions: Write the correct division word for each definition. Then write an example division problem for that word.

Word	Definition	Example
	The number that is divided in a division problem.	
	The number by which a number is being divided.	
	A word describing a number that can be divided equally by another, resulting in a whole number with no remainder.	
	The answer of a division problem.	
	The number leftover after dividing one number by another.	
	A word that describes a pair of numbers easy to work with mentally and used in place of actual numbers to estimate division.	
	A word that describes the relationship of multiplication to division.	
	The process by which a larger place value is traded for equal numbers of a smaller place value.	
	A word that describes any of these symbols: +, −, ×, ÷.	
	A mathematical sentence showing the relationship of two equal expressions using numbers and symbols.	

DIVISIBILITY DASH

Objective

Students will use divisibility rules to determine the factors of greater numbers in a relay race.

Anticipatory Set

Write "1,237,365,289,516" on the board, and ask students to raise their hands if they think that the number is divisible by 4. Ask, "How would you like to do long division to prove it?" Then ask, "Who would like to learn a quick way to figure out the answer without doing long division or using a calculator?"

Purpose

Explain to students that there are situations in which they will need to quickly know if a large number is divisible by a certain factor. For example, without using long division, how could they determine if 148 cookies can be distributed equally into nine bags for a bake sale? Explain that *divisibility rules* can help them determine whether a large whole number is divisible by another. Tell students that they will learn these rules and use them to run a relay race.

Input

Remind students that a whole number is *divisible* by another if there is no remainder after the division. In that case, the second number (*divisor*) is a *factor* of the first number (*dividend*).

Display the following divisibility rules, and review them with students. Explain that these rules provide quick methods for finding factors of greater numbers. Point out the similarities in the rules for 3 and 9 and for 5 and 10. Have students write the rules and examples in their math journals, or give them photocopies.

Divisibility Rules

- **2:** A number is divisible by 2 if it is an even number (ending in 0, 2, 4, 6, or 8).

Example: 394 is divisible by 2 because it is an even number (it ends with 4).

- **3:** A number is divisible by 3 if the sum of its digits is divisible by 3.

Example: 828 is divisible by 3 because 8 + 2 + 8 = 18, which is divisible by 3.

- **4:** A number is divisible by 4 if the last two digits together are divisible by 4.

Example: 512 is divisible by 4 because 12 is divisible by 4.

- **5:** A number is divisible by 5 if it ends with 0 or 5.

Example: 79,345 is divisible by 5 because it ends with 5.

- **6:** A number is divisible by 6 if it is also divisible by both 2 and 3.

Example: 15,834 is divisible by 6 because it is also divisible by 2 and 3 (15,834 is an even number; 1 + 5 + 8 + 3 + 4 = 21).

- **8:** A number is divisible by 8 if the last three digits together are divisible by 8.

Example: 193,184 is divisible by 8 because 184 is divisible by 8.

- **9:** A number is divisible by 9 if the sum of its digits is divisible by 9.

Example: 828 is divisible by 9 because 8 + 2 + 8 = 18, which is divisible by 9.

- **10:** A number is divisible by 10 if it ends with 0.

Example: 79,340 is divisible by 10 because it ends with 0.

Point out that a number can have more than one of the factors listed above. For example, 79,340 is divisible by both 5 and 10.

Modeling

Ask students, "How could we use connecting cubes to prove that 24 is divisible by 2, 3, 4, 6, and 8?"

Model how to take a stick of 24 connected cubes and break it (divide it) into pairs to make 12 equal groups with no remainder, proving that 24 is divisible by 2. Write, "24 ÷ 2 = 12 pairs with no remainder, so 24 is divisible by 2." Invite volunteers to demonstrate how to repeat the process for the numbers *3, 4, 6,* and *8* to prove that 24 is divisible by all of them.

Then ask, "How could we use grid paper to prove that 160 is divisible by 2, 5, and 10?" Demonstrate the process of outlining a set of 160 grid squares and then coloring by groups of 2, 5, or 10 to prove that 160 is divisible by all of those numbers.

Checking for Understanding

The use of various models is important because relying on just one model may not be sufficient.

Ask students, "If you want to prove that 828 is divisible by 2, 3, 6, and 9, which method would you use: connecting cubes, grid paper, long division, or divisibility rules? Why?" (*divisibility rules because it is the quickest method*).

Guided Practice

Tell students that they can use divisibility rules to help them play a relay race. They will be racing to retrieve posted multidigit numbers that are divisible by factors you call out. The first player to return with a correct answer earns two points. The other players earn one point for a correct answer. The team with the most points at the end of the game wins.

Demonstrate how to play the game by posting on a wall the numbers 19,482, 64,836, and 50,270, written on separate sheets of paper. Then ask students the following questions:

- If I call out "9," which number would you grab off the wall? Why? (*64,836. It is the only number divisible by 9 because 6 + 4 + 8 + 3 + 6 = 27.*).
- If I call out "2," which number could you grab? Why? (*I could grab any of the numbers because they are all even numbers.*).
- If I call out both "2" and "4," which number is the only one you could grab? Why? (*64,836. It is the only even number with the last two digits divisible by 4.*).

Independent Practice

Write the following numbers (excluding answers in parentheses) on separate sheets of paper. Tape them to a wall outside the classroom for a relay race (you may choose to reapply them after each round of the game).

9,060 (2, 3, 4, 5, 6, 10)   5,944 (2, 4, 8)

9,675 (3, 5, 9)   2,736 (2, 3, 4, 6, 8, 9)

6,200 (2, 4, 5, 8, 10)   6,480 (2, 3, 4, 5, 6, 8, 9, 10)

2,424 (2, 3, 4, 6, 8)   9,112 (2, 4, 8)

5,070 (2, 3, 5, 6, 10)   3,126 (2, 3, 6)

1,890 (2, 3, 5, 6, 9, 10)   3,012 (2, 3, 4, 6)

6,765 (3, 5)   1,728 (2, 3, 4, 6, 8, 9)

2,744 (2, 4, 8)   4,320 (2, 3, 4, 5, 6, 8, 9, 10)

Divide the class into four or five teams, and ask teams to line up single file behind a starting line. Then have teammates take turns racing to the wall to retrieve a number that is divisible by a factor you call out. They earn two points (first team with correct answer), one point (correct answer but not the first team), or no points (wrong answer). Start with single factors, and then increase the challenge by calling out factor pairs, trios, or quartets. Remind students to use the divisibility rules to help find correct answers as quickly as possible.

Closure

Ask students to answer the following questions in their math journals: "What math skills did you learn today? How can those skills help you in the future, both in math class and outside of school?"

SCUBA DIVISION

Objective

Students will work in cooperative groups using their division and other math skills to write and solve word problems about scuba diving.

Anticipatory Set

Gain students' attention by having them join you in creating a folded paper project. Have students follow along as you demonstrate each step:

1. Fold the paper in half lengthwise and vertically, and then open it to show two creases.

2. Draw a wavy line along the horizontal crease, and draw a straight line down the vertical crease.

3. Use the vertical line to make a number line, writing "0" at the point at which it crosses the wavy line. Write positive numbers upward from 0 at equal intervals of 10 and negative numbers downward.

Ask students, "What do you think we are going to learn in math class today?" Allow students to respond, and then write "Scuba Division" on the board.

Purpose

Explain to students that the word *scuba* stands for "self-contained underwater breathing apparatus" and involves the use of specialized equipment that helps divers stay underwater for long periods of time. Point out that scuba diving is used in a variety of professions, including oceanography, photography, coast guarding, and underwater rescue. In this activity, students will use their division skills and other math skills to write and solve word problems about scuba diving.

Input

Give each student a copy of the **Scuba Diving Facts and Figures reproducible (page 35).** Read the reproducible aloud. Suggest that students inhale deeply to feel their lungs expand and exhale to feel their lungs contract and deflate. Point out that if someone were sitting on a student's chest or hugging him or her tightly, much like the effects of water pressure on a scuba diver, it would be much harder for the student to expand his or her lungs and breathe.

Encourage students to ask questions about scuba diving. Remind them that the ocean is home to a variety of life forms, including schools of fish, pools of plankton, sharks, whales, and thousands of other marine animals. If possible, show pictures of the ocean and scuba divers exploring the aquatic environment.

Then tell students that they will use their Scuba Diving Facts and Figures sheets and four-section papers to write scuba diving problems (one per section) for classmates to solve. List and discuss the following criteria for the problems:

- All of the problems must be word problems about scuba diving or the ocean.
- At least two problems must involve division and dividends greater than three digits.
- At least one problem must be a multistep problem.
- At least one problem must involve addition or subtraction of negative numbers.
- At least one problem must involve the use of number patterns.

Modeling

Model how to use the vertical number line to add and subtract positive and negative numbers as students follow along on their own number lines. (You might encourage them to move counters along their number lines.) For example, ask the following questions:

- A scuba diver drops to a depth of 10 ft/m below sea level. Then she dives down 20 ft/m more. At what depth is she now? $(-10 + -20 = -30 \, ft/m)$.
- A scuba diver is at 50 ft/m below sea level. He ascends 20 ft/m. At what depth is he now? $(-50 + 20 = -30 \, ft/m)$.

Then demonstrate how to solve a problem using patterns and mental math. For example, "How can you use the fact $36 \div 12$ and patterns of zero to determine how many times deeper the Marianas Trench is compared to the average ocean depth?" (*Use stacked division and cross off common zeros, multiples of ten, to show that the Marianas Trench is three times deeper: $36,000 \, ft/m \div 12,000 \, ft/m = 36,\cancel{000} \, ft/m \div 12,\cancel{000} \, ft/m = 36 \, ft/m \div 12 \, ft/m = 3$ times deeper.*).

> Model the enjoyment of numbers and number patterns. Creating and using conceptual subitizing patterns helps children develop abstract number and arithmetic strategies.

Guided Practice

Guide students as they write four division problems. Circulate around the room to answer any questions and to check that students are writing their problems correctly, one problem per section. Ask each student to include a separate answer key on another sheet of paper that shows the solution for each problem.

Remind students to refer to the listed criteria and their Scuba Diving Facts and Figures sheet. Encourage them to refer to your examples. You might also permit them to use calculators. If some students finish early, invite them work on a picture or cartoon about scuba diving that illustrates one of their problems.

Divide the class into groups of four, and have group members exchange papers (or assign students to groups according to mixed ability levels). Tell students that they will have 5 minutes to solve one of the four problems on the papers they receive. When you say time is up, they should exchange papers again and solve a problem on the next sheets they receive. They may choose any remaining problem. But before they begin, they must check and correct any mistakes made on the previously completed problem. Students should cross out mistakes (not erase) and write the correct answers. Direct students to write their initials next to each problem they solve as well as any corrections they make to someone else's work.

Checking for Understanding

Invite a group to demonstrate how to exchange papers within the group, rotating the papers clockwise around the circle. Remind students that you will announce that time is up four times, every 5 minutes. Point out that for the last round, each student will solve the final problem on his or her own paper.

Independent Practice

Start the clock, and invite students to begin. After 5 minutes, tell them that time is up and to rotate papers within their groups. Repeat the process three more times until each group has completed the four problems on each paper.

Closure

Have students use their answer keys to check and critique the work completed on their math papers. Invite them to discuss the results and provide feedback. If students disagree on an answer, ask the whole group to work together to rework the problem and determine the correct answer.

Scuba Diving Facts and Figures

- The average depth of an ocean is about 12,000 feet (3,657.60 meters). But some trenches, such as the Marianas Trench, can reach a depth of almost 36,000 feet (10,972.80 meters).

- Open-water scuba divers descend to about 60 feet below sea level (8.29 meters). Deep-sea divers descend to about 120 feet below sea level (36.58 meters).

- As a diver descends into the ocean, the water applies increasing pressure of about 1 bar per 30 feet of depth (100,000 pascals per 9.14 meters). This makes it harder for the diver to breathe, as if he or she is being squeezed. Divers must use a diving regulator to get breathing gas from a cylinder. The gas has equal pressure to the surrounding water pressure. This helps the diver to inhale and exhale naturally. The deeper the dive, the greater the pressure and the more oxygen used.

- Water conducts heat 25 times better than air. Scuba divers should wear a diving suit that lessens heat loss to avoid a "chilling" condition called hypothermia. Some suits can also be inflated to reduce the "squeeze" caused by increased pressure. These suits have vents that allow excess air to escape on ascent.

- Scuba divers often wear a belt of lead weights to counteract the force pushing them upward so they can move downward. This force is called buoyancy. The diver's positive buoyancy determines the number of weights. Positive buoyancy depends on the diver's body makeup. It also includes the buoyancy of the diving suit and gear worn, water salt, and water temperature. Divers often wear 4 to 30 pounds (1.81 to 13.61 kilograms) of weights. In an emergency, divers can drop weights to provide instant buoyancy and a quick ascent to the surface.

- Decompression illness (DCI) results from nitrogen bubbles that form inside the diver's blood or tissue because of changing pressure. To reduce the risk of DCI, divers should ascend slowly back to the surface. They should move no faster than 30 feet (9.14 meters) per minute. Divers should also stop once in a while to give absorbed nitrogen bubbles time to be exhaled from the lungs at reduced pressure.

SHOW THE ORDER

Objective

Students will use the order of operations to simplify and solve math problems.

Anticipatory Set

Ask students if they have ever been confused by instructions for making or doing something, such as a recipe or a game. Explain that complicated instructions can be broken down into smaller steps to make the task more manageable.

Display the following example for the class. Explain that one answer is correct and the other is incorrect: $(42 - 12) \div (3 + 3) + (2 \times 5) = 75$ or 15. Ask students to whisper to their neighbors the answer they think is correct. Tell them that they will learn how to break down this and other problems like this into smaller steps to find the correct answer.

Purpose

Tell students that they should always use the *order of operations* to simplify complex math expressions. Compare it to simplifying a wordy sentence such as "I enjoy the presence of your company" to "I like you." In this activity, student teams will simplify and solve math problems using the order of operations.

Input

> Process mnemonics are powerful memory devices that help students with mathematics difficulties learn basic arithmetic operations.

Display the following rules for the order of operations, and have students copy them into their math journals. You might also have students refer to the mnemonic device "**P**lease **E**xcuse **M**y **D**ear **A**unt **S**ally" to help them remember the order. Invite students to offer other mnemonic devices that could help their classmates.

Order of Operations

1. Simplify the terms within **parentheses.**

2. Simplify the terms with **exponents.**

4. **Multiply** and **divide** from left to right.

5. **Add** and **subtract** from left to right.

Modeling

Use a transparency of the **Order of Operations Chart reproducible (page 39)** to demonstrate how to simplify a complex math expression step by step. Have students copy the following example in their math journals:

$$(7^2 + 6) \div (19 - 8) \cdot 4 \Rightarrow$$
$$(49 + 6) \div (19 - 8) \cdot 4 \Rightarrow$$
$$55 \div 11 \cdot 4 \Rightarrow$$
$$5 \cdot 4 \Rightarrow$$
$$20$$

Point out that the associative property (which states that you can move parentheses and regroup without changing the sum or product) applies only to an expression that contains all addition or all multiplication, not a combination of operations. For example, $(5 + 4) + 2 = 5 + (4 + 2)$, but $(5 \cdot 4) + 2 \neq 5 \cdot (4 + 2)$.

Then show students another math expression to simplify, such as $(9 - 5)^3 - (6 \cdot 4) \div 2$. This time, have students help you decide which operation to use at each step either by writing the operation on individual white boards or by holding up one of six word cards they have made: *addition, subtraction, multiplication, division, parentheses,* and *exponent.* For example,

$$(9 - 5)^3 - (6 \cdot 4) \div 2 \Rightarrow \text{parentheses}$$
$$4^3 - (6 \cdot 4) \div 2 \Rightarrow \text{parentheses}$$
$$4^3 - 24 \div 2 \Rightarrow \text{exponent}$$
$$64 - 24 \div 2 \Rightarrow \text{division}$$
$$64 - 12 \Rightarrow \text{subtraction}$$
$$52$$

After showing students how to simplify numerical expressions, demonstrate how to simplify algebraic expressions, such as $(2x + 6y) \div x$, given $x = 3$ and $y = 5$. Plug in the values for x and y, and then use the order of operations to solve (*12*). Again, ask students to help you decide the correct order of operations.

Checking for Understanding

Ask students to recite chorally the rules for the order of operations. Remind them always to follow these rules when simplifying an expression and to check that they simplify the expression completely. (Suggest that they cross off each part and rewrite the expression after each step.) Then refer to the expression and two answers given at the beginning of the lesson. Invite a volunteer to show the solution step by step, and ask the class to check his or her work. Confirm the correct answer (*15*).

Guided Practice

Divide the class into teams of three or four students, and give each team several Order of Operations Charts and two sets of operation cards (*addition, subtraction, multiplication, division, parentheses,* and *exponent*). Explain that you will show them an expression to simplify, and the team must stand in a row using the word cards to show the correct order of operations for the solution. Then they must simplify and solve the expression. For example, for

$3 \cdot (9 - 3) + 5$, the operation cards are *parentheses, multiplication,* and *addition* for an answer of 23.

The first team with the correct solution wins one point. The team with the most points at the end of the game wins. Use the following math problems for the game, starting with the simpler expressions and increasing the level of difficulty to include algebra. Have teams rotate the role of "recorder," who writes the sequence of steps for each solution.

$4 + (24 \div 6) \cdot 8$ (Correct order: *p, m, a;* answer = 36)

$14 - 3 \cdot (2 + 1)$ (Correct order: *p, m s;* answer = 5)

$(6 \cdot 4) - 3^2 + (2 \cdot 8)$ (Correct order: *p, p, e, s, a;* answer = 31)

$20 - 12 \div 4 + 5 + 3 \cdot 5$ (Correct order: *d, m, s, a, a;* answer = 37)

$(2x + 3y) - y$, given $x = 3$, $y = 5$ (Correct order: *p, a, s;* answer: = 16)

$16 + (x - 4) \div y^2$, given $x = 8$, $y = 2$ (Correct order: *p, x, d;* answer = 17)

Closure

Prompt students to discuss the skills and strategies they used to play the game and share how their teams were successful (or not) at working together. Invite them to write about their experiences in their math journals.

Independent Practice

Have students complete the **Show the Order reproducible (page 40).** Remind them to follow the order of operations and simplify. Before collecting the papers, have partners compare answers and rework any errors together.

Name_____ Date_____

Order of Operations Chart

Directions: Write and simplify a math expression using the order of operations: parentheses, exponents, multiplication or division, addition or subtraction.

Expression

Name _____   Date _____

Show the Order

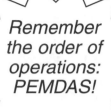

Remember the order of operations: PEMDAS!

Directions: Use the order of operations to simplify and solve.

1. Insert parentheses so this expression equals 17.

   $2 \cdot 6 + 5 - 18 \div 2 + 2^2$

2. Write a math expression that equals 16 and uses only 24, 8, 4, and 2 in that order.

3. Simplify $100 \div x^2 + 3(y - x)$, given $x = 2$ and $y = 6$.

4. There are 112 customers in a restaurant. Then 4 groups of 6 customers leave, and 3 groups of 5 more come in. How many customers are there now?

Math Expression: _____

Step-by-Step Solution:

5. A team of chefs must prepare 168 meals for their customers. The first chef prepares 6 groups of 5 meals. The second chef prepares half the number of meals as the first chef. The third chef prepares three times the number of meals as the second chef. The last chef prepares 19 meals. How many meals are left to prepare?

Math Expression: _____

Step-by-Step Solution:

Write Your Own Problem

On the back of this paper, write and solve your own complex math problem about a store or restaurant. Use the order of operations.

2

Fractions and Decimals

Fraction Friends

Fun With Fractions

Decimal Days

Put the Dot on the Spot

Dollars and Sense

A Portrait of Parts

Grocery Bill Math

Party Planners

Fraction Cooking

Calling All Construction Workers

FRACTION FRIENDS

Objective

Students will learn to identify fractions by exploring different models.

Anticipatory Set

Invite three boys and two girls to stand together at the front of the class. Encourage students to think about the boys and girls in the group. Ask, "Is there a way you can describe parts of this group using numbers?" Even though there might be a variety of answers, guide the discussion toward the conclusion that three of the five are boys and two of the five are girls.

Purpose

Students are already experienced in working with whole numbers such as *one, two,* and *five.* Tell them, "A *fraction* is a number that describes the equal parts of a whole." Point to the five students standing in the group. Ask, "If the whole group has five parts in it, how many parts of the group are boys?" (*three out of five*). Tell students that they will be working with parts of a whole, or fractions.

Input

Draw a pie chart on the board. Divide it into five equal parts. Say, "If we draw a model of this group to show how many parts of the group are boys, we shade in three parts of the circle." Shade in three sections of the pie chart.

Explain that this drawing can be written as $^3/_5$, and write it on the board next to the pie chart. Say, "The bottom number in a fraction, the *denominator,* tells the total number in the whole group." Ask a volunteer to identify the denominator (5). Continue: "The top number in a fraction, the *numerator,* tells the number of parts." Ask a volunteer to identify the numerator (3).

Modeling

To demonstrate more fraction models, invite a different group of students to the front of the room—four girls and four boys. Count the number with students, and ask, "How many students are in this whole group?" Draw a pie chart, and divide it into eight equal parts. Ask, "How many girls are in this group?" Shade in four sections of the pie chart. Write the fraction $^4/_8$ on the board next to the chart. Ask volunteers to identify the denominator and the numerator.

Continue to ask a variety of groups to help you model fractions. For example, use students who are wearing different shoes or have different colors of hair.

Checking for Understanding

Check to make sure everyone knows how to write a fraction. Draw a picture on the board representing a fraction. Have students write the fraction on a piece of paper and show it to their neighbors. Then write the fraction on the board. Have students check their neighbors' answers. Repeat this activity as needed.

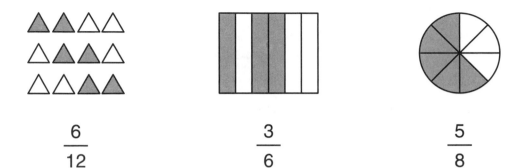

$$\frac{6}{12} \qquad \frac{3}{6} \qquad \frac{5}{8}$$

Guided Practice

Tell students that they will perform a read-aloud play to continue practice with identifying fractions. Distribute copies of the **Planets for Sale reproducibles (pages 44–46),** and assign parts. Every student should have a part in the play, either as a main character or as part of a group. Read the play together. When finished, praise students for their participation.

> Remember that all students benefit when they use a variety of modalities while learning.

Closure

Draw a pie chart on the board representing each planet in the play. Remind students that a fraction is a number that describes the equal parts of a whole. Shade in part of each planet, and ask volunteers to write the matching fraction on the board. When finished, invite each student to draw a picture of his or her favorite planet from the play in his or her math journal. Instruct students to retell the play in their own words in their journals as if they were looking for a planet to buy.

Independent Practice

Divide the class into small groups. Ask each group to create its own model of a fraction using the boys and girls in the group. Instruct each group to work together to use circles, triangles, or squares to draw a picture of its fraction on a piece of paper and write the fraction beside the picture. Then take time for each group to share its fraction with the class.

Planets for Sale

A Play About Fractions

Narrator: Deep in the remote regions of outer space, in a galaxy far, far away, a family of three aliens walked into a realtor's office.

Mr. Alien: We are looking to buy a new home. Do you have any planets for sale?

Realtor: Planets for cheap or planets for more—I've got just the right planet for you!

Mrs. Alien: The planet I want has to be the right size. Not just any planet will do.

Realtor: How big do you want it to be?

Alien Junior: I want my own room.

Mrs. Alien: I want an office to use for my new business.

Mr. Alien: I want a room where I can sit each night and read the *Alien News.*

Realtor: Great! Let's take a look around. I'll show you the newest listings.

Narrator: The group zoomed off together in a spaceship. Soon they came to a stop.

Realtor: This is the Planet of **HALVES.** You get double the fun because there is room for two of everything on this planet! You can even have two swimming pools.

Mr. Alien: Two swimming pools! But what would the neighbors think?

Alien Junior: But it's not big enough! I wouldn't have my own room.

Mrs. Alien: That's right. It does look too small. Do you have any other planets for sale?

Realtor: Sure. Just past this small moon.

Narrator: The group zoomed off and stopped in front of another planet.

Planets for Sale (Continued)

Realtor:	This is the Planet of **EIGHTHS.** The family hasn't moved out yet.
Mr. Alien:	That's strange. This planet looks like a pizza.
Mrs. Alien:	And the people look like pepperoni.
Alien Junior:	And it smells like stinky cheese!
Realtor:	Well, this is the biggest planet listed for sale.
Narrator:	The realtor and the alien family stepped onto the Planet of Eighths.
Family of Eighths (group reading):	Careful! Watch your step!
Realtor:	Mind if we come in and look around?
Family of Eighths:	Go ahead. Take a look. Just don't step on us.
Mrs. Alien:	Ugh! The carpet is covered with cheese.
Alien Junior:	This place is huge!
Mr. Alien:	What would we do with five extra rooms? Do you have any other planets for sale?
Realtor:	Of course I do. Let's fly to the next place on my listings.
Family of Eighths:	Good-bye!
Narrator:	With that, the group zoomed off. They stopped in front of another planet.
Realtor:	This is the Planet of **FOURTHS.** Meet the Fourths family!
Mr. Alien:	This looks more like it! My very own swimming pool!

Planets for Sale (Continued)

Family of Fourths (group reading): If you like to swim, you'll love our planet.

Mrs. Alien: But the whole planet is covered with water! What about my business?

Family of Fourths: Start a brand new business. You could open a water park!

Alien Junior: Our very own water park! I could invite all my friends.

Mrs. Alien: No! I will not live in a swimming pool.

Mr. Alien: Yes, and it is still a little too large. I don't think it is right for our family. We are on a budget, you know!

Realtor: I do have one last planet for sale. Would you like to take a look at it?

Mr. and Mrs. Alien: Yes, let's take a look.

Narrator: The group zoomed off to look at one more planet.

Realtor: This is the Planet of **THIRDS.** Take a look around. Let me know if you like it.

Mrs. Alien: Look, this planet is divided into three equal parts. That means you will have a place to sit and read, I will have my office, and Junior will get his own room. We'll take it! It's perfect!

Mr. Alien: It does seem to be everything that we have been looking for.

Alien Junior: I even get my own room!

Realtor: Sold!

Narrator: And the family of three aliens lived happily every after on the Planet of THIRDS.

FUN WITH FRACTIONS

Objective

Students will work with number lines and models to identify equivalent fractions.

Anticipatory Set

Draw four circles on the board. Divide one circle into halves, one into fourths, one into sixths, and one into eighths. Shade in one half of each circle's parts, as shown. Write the fractions under the matching circles: ¹/₂, ²/₄, ³/₆, and ⁴/₈. Invite students to think about the examples. Ask, "Are these fractions the same or different?"

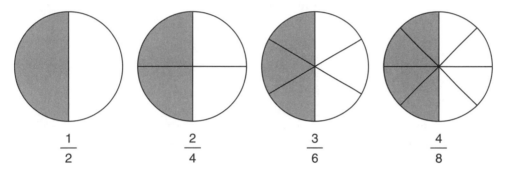

$$\frac{1}{2} \qquad \frac{2}{4} \qquad \frac{3}{6} \qquad \frac{4}{8}$$

Purpose

Tell students that they will be comparing fractions with the same value.

Input

Tell students that different fractions can represent the same part of a whole. These are called *equivalent fractions*. Equivalent fractions name the same part. The fractions ¹/₂, ²/₄, ³/₆, and ⁴/₈ are equivalent fractions.

Give each student a copy of the **Equivalent Fractions Mat reproducible (page 50).** Place a transparency of the reproducible on the overhead. Instruct students to examine the number lines on the mat as they listen and follow along.

Ask students, "How are all the number lines the same?" Allow students to respond, and then point out that each number line goes from 0 to 1. Ask, "How is each number line different?" Explain that each number line represents different fractions. Count the fractions on each number line together in unison from 0 to 1.

Instruct students to examine the strips on the right side of the mat. Ask them to compare and contrast each set of strips. Point out that the strips and the number lines both represent the same fractions and the whole number *1*. Explain that using the mat will help them to identify equivalent fractions.

Modeling

Place an unmarked transparency over the transparency of the reproducible. Use a red marker to draw a line on the unmarked transparency from 0 to

1 over the first number line. Write the number *1* above the red line. Then reposition the red line, and move it down so that it is positioned on top of the second number line. Ask students, "How many halves are equivalent to the number *1?*" Invite a volunteer to share the answer ($\frac{2}{2}$). Above the red line, write "$1 = \frac{2}{2}$." Then reposition the red line so it is on top of the next number line. Ask, "How many fourths are equivalent to the number *1?*" Invite a volunteer to share the answer ($\frac{4}{4}$). Above the red line, write "$1 = \frac{2}{2} = \frac{4}{4}$." Explain that $\frac{2}{2}$ and $\frac{4}{4}$ are equivalent fractions.

Repeat this activity by placing the red line on top of each number line. Each time, write the equations to show the equivalent fractions. Then move the red line to the right side of the mat, and cover the top strip, the strips representing halves, and so on until you have located all the equivalent fractions for 1.

Wipe off the red line, and draw a new line on the unmarked transparency from 0 to $\frac{1}{2}$ on the second number line. Model how to find equivalent fractions for $\frac{1}{2}$ by moving the red line onto the various number lines and strips. Repeat this activity for as many fractions as possible. As you work, stop to demonstrate with pairs of equivalent fractions that you can multiply or divide both the numerator and denominator by the same number to prove that the numbers are equivalent fractions.

Checking for Understanding

Turn off the overhead, and ask students to look at their own mats to answer review questions such as, *Name an equivalent fraction for $\frac{1}{2}$.* Instruct students to whisper their answers to neighbors, and then invite a volunteer to share the answer.

Guided Practice

Divide the class into small groups of four or five students. Give each student the following supplies: one toilet tissue cardboard tube (or paper towel tube cut in half), one 5×10 in piece of gift wrap, and two 10-in pieces of narrow ribbon. Give each group glue and clear tape. In the center of each group, place a small bowl containing an assortment of individually wrapped hard candies, balloons, stickers, or other small treats that fit inside the tube.

Use index cards to create a set of equivalent fraction cards. Write the following fraction equivalences, one on each card:

$\frac{2}{3} = \frac{}{6}$	$\frac{2}{2} = \frac{}{4}$	$\frac{1}{3} = \frac{}{12}$	$\frac{2}{6} = \frac{}{12}$
$\frac{2}{4} = \frac{}{8}$	$\frac{4}{8} = \frac{}{4}$	$\frac{6}{8} = \frac{}{4}$	$\frac{1}{4} = \frac{}{12}$
$\frac{10}{12} = \frac{}{6}$	$\frac{3}{4} = \frac{}{8}$	$\frac{12}{12} = \frac{}{8}$	$\frac{1}{2} = \frac{}{8}$
$\frac{2}{3} = \frac{}{12}$	$\frac{1}{2} = \frac{}{6}$	$\frac{3}{3} = \frac{}{6}$	$\frac{8}{12} = \frac{}{6}$

Distribute one card to each student. Instruct each student to determine the equivalent fraction on his or her card. Encourage students to refer to their mats as needed. Then have them choose the corresponding number of treats from the bowl to place on their squares of gift wrap. This number represents the answer for the missing numerator.

Have group members check each other's work. When everyone has the correct answer, tell students to return the items to the bowl, exchange cards within their group, and solve their new equations by placing the correct number of items on their squares of gift wrap.

Repeat this process several times, having group members work together to check and correct each other's work. When they are done practicing, have students keep their last cards and the accompanying treats. Explain that they will be making party poppers to give away at a math party.

Show students how to make a party popper:

> Activities that are challenging and meaningful not only develop students' cognitive strengths but also raise motivation and, thus, enhance the enjoyment of learning mathematics.

1. Place the correct number of items inside the cardboard tube.

2. Cover the tube with gift wrap and tape.

3. Tie the ends with ribbon.

4. Glue the index card to the outside of the popper.

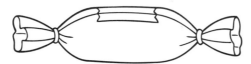

Independent Practice

Collect all the poppers. Tell students that you will save them for a celebration the following day. For homework, have students refer to their Equivalent Fractions Mat reproducibles. Tell them to write as many pairs of equivalent fractions as they can find represented on the mat.

Closure

The next day, after collecting students' homework, distribute the poppers to celebrate how well students have learned fractions. Invite each student to solve the equation on his or her popper, open the popper, and count the objects inside to check the answer. Then allow students to enjoy the treats. Later, ask them to reflect on the activity in their math journals. Encourage them to write the most important thing they learned about equivalent fractions.

Extending the Activity

Have parent volunteers make each student a set of fraction strips. Cut 1×12 in (2.54×30.48 cm) strips of construction paper into equal parts to represent different fractions. Use different-colored paper for each set of fractions (e.g., 2 orange strips for halves, 3 blue strips for thirds, 5 red strips for fifths, and 10 yellow strips for tenths). Allow time for students to practice finding equivalent fractions using their fraction strips.

Equivalent Fractions Mat

Strips

1			
$\frac{1}{2}$		$\frac{1}{2}$	
$\frac{1}{4}$	$\frac{1}{4}$	$\frac{1}{4}$	$\frac{1}{4}$
$\frac{1}{8}$ $\frac{1}{8}$	$\frac{1}{8}$ $\frac{1}{8}$	$\frac{1}{8}$ $\frac{1}{8}$	$\frac{1}{8}$ $\frac{1}{8}$

1		
$\frac{1}{3}$	$\frac{1}{3}$	$\frac{1}{3}$
$\frac{1}{6}$ $\frac{1}{6}$	$\frac{1}{6}$ $\frac{1}{6}$	$\frac{1}{6}$ $\frac{1}{6}$
$\frac{1}{12}$ $\frac{1}{12}$ $\frac{1}{12}$ $\frac{1}{12}$	$\frac{1}{12}$ $\frac{1}{12}$ $\frac{1}{12}$ $\frac{1}{12}$	$\frac{1}{12}$ $\frac{1}{12}$ $\frac{1}{12}$ $\frac{1}{12}$

Number Lines

Number line: 0 to 1

Number line: $\frac{0}{2}$, $\frac{1}{2}$, $\frac{2}{2}$

Number line: $\frac{0}{4}$, $\frac{1}{4}$, $\frac{2}{4}$, $\frac{3}{4}$, $\frac{4}{4}$

Number line: $\frac{0}{8}$, $\frac{1}{8}$, $\frac{2}{8}$, $\frac{3}{8}$, $\frac{4}{8}$, $\frac{5}{8}$, $\frac{6}{8}$, $\frac{7}{8}$, $\frac{8}{8}$

Number line: 0 to 1

Number line: $\frac{0}{3}$, $\frac{1}{3}$, $\frac{2}{3}$, $\frac{3}{3}$

Number line: $\frac{0}{6}$, $\frac{1}{6}$, $\frac{2}{6}$, $\frac{3}{6}$, $\frac{4}{6}$, $\frac{5}{6}$, $\frac{6}{6}$

Number line: $\frac{0}{12}$, $\frac{1}{12}$, $\frac{2}{12}$, $\frac{3}{12}$, $\frac{4}{12}$, $\frac{5}{12}$, $\frac{6}{12}$, $\frac{7}{12}$, $\frac{8}{12}$, $\frac{9}{12}$, $\frac{10}{12}$, $\frac{11}{12}$, $\frac{12}{12}$

DECIMAL DAYS

Objective

Students will work with models and play a card game to review how fractions are related to decimals.

Anticipatory Set

Show students a dollar bill and a dime. Tell them, "This bill is worth one whole dollar. A dime is worth one tenth of one dollar." On the board, draw a rectangle to represent the dollar. Divide it into 10 equal columns. Shade in the first column to represent the dime. Write the fraction $1/10$ next to the rectangle.

Tell students that another way to write a fraction is as a decimal: "If a fraction has a denominator of 10 or 100, you can also write it as a decimal." On the board, write "0.10." Point out that the fraction $1/10$ and the decimal 0.10 represent the same amount. Decimals are used to write dollars and cents. Ask volunteers to suggest other situations in which people might use decimals instead of fractions (*to time a race at the Olympics, to show a person's weight on a digital scale, to weigh fruits and vegetables, and so on*).

Purpose

Tell students that understanding how fractions are related to decimals is an important math concept. In this activity, they will work with models and then play a game to help them gain a deeper understanding of this concept.

Input

Place a transparency of the **Decimal Days reproducible (page 53)** on the overhead. Count aloud together the number of columns in the top grid. Explain, "This model is divided into tenths, or 10 equal parts." Shade in the first column in the top grid and say, "The shaded part is one tenth." Write the fraction $1/10$ in the box to the right of the grid. Write the decimal 0.1.

Show students the bottom grid and say, "This model is divided into hundredths, or 100 equal parts." Shade in the first column in the bottom grid. Tell students, "The shaded part is 10 hundredths." Write the fraction $10/100$ in the box to the right of the grid. Write the decimal 0.10.

Ask students to think about and compare the two grids. Guide a discussion to help them understand that each example on the reproducible is a different way to name or model the same number.

Modeling

Erase the fractions and decimals in the two boxes. Then shade in the second column in the top grid. Tell students, "The shaded part is now two tenths." Invite a volunteer to write the fraction $2/10$ and the decimal 0.2 in the boxes. Now shade in the second column in the bottom grid. Tell students, "The shaded part is now 20 hundredths." Invite a volunteer to write the fraction $^{20}/_{100}$ and the decimal *0.20* in the boxes. Continue to model shading in the columns for both grids. Each time, write the fraction and decimal in the boxes.

Checking for Understanding

Remind students that if a fraction has a denominator of 10 or 100, it can also be written as a decimal. Wipe the transparency, and then shade in the first two columns on both grids. Ask students to write the fraction and the decimal for each. Check that everyone answers correctly. Model more examples if needed.

Guided Practice

Tell students that they will play a card game to practice identifying related fractions and decimals. Divide the class into teams of four or five students. Copy the **Decimal Days Game Cards reproducibles (pages 54–56),** and give each group one set of cards. (Cards may be glued to index cards or laminated for durability.)

The Decimal Days card game is played similarly to Go Fish. First, instruct each group to shuffle the cards and deal six cards to each player. Player 1 asks any other player (player 2) if he or she has a certain card, such as, *Do you have twenty hundredths?* Player 1 must already be holding one card from that set. If player 2 has one or both of these cards, he or she must give them to player 1, and player 1 gets another turn. If not, player 1 must draw a card from the draw pile, and play moves to the next player.

If a player collects a three-card set (fraction, decimal, and word cards), he or she places the cards faceup on the table and scores one point. If the same player collects two complete sets of the same value (such as three tenths and thirty hundredths), those cards count double, and the player scores four points. The player with the most points at the end of the game wins.

Closure

Invite students to share strategies they used to help them remember how fractions and decimals are related. Prompt them to write in their math journals about how learning to work with decimals can help them when they go to the store.

Independent Practice

Give each student a copy of the Decimal Days reproducible, and assign a different fraction to each student. Some students may have the same fraction. For homework, instruct them to shade in each model to show the fraction and the related fraction and then write both corresponding fractions and decimals.

Name_____ Date_____

Decimal Days

Directions: Write the name of your fraction: _____

Shade in the models. Write the matching fractions and decimals.

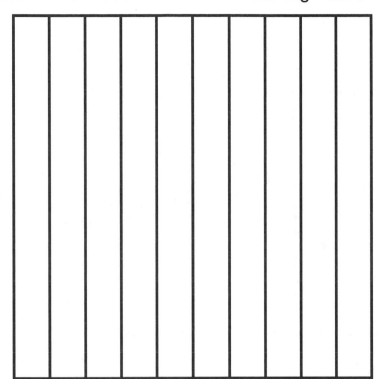

Fraction
Decimal

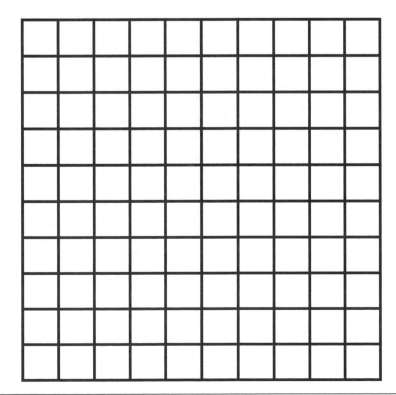

Fraction
Decimal

Decimal Days Game Cards

$\dfrac{1}{10}$	one tenth		$\dfrac{2}{10}$
0.2	two tenths	0.1	0.3
three tenths	$\dfrac{4}{10}$	$\dfrac{3}{10}$	four tenths
$\dfrac{5}{10}$	five tenths	0.4	$\dfrac{6}{10}$
0.6	six tenths	0.5	0.7
		$\dfrac{7}{10}$	

Decimal Days Game Cards

eight tenths	0.8	seven tenths
$\frac{10}{10}$	nine tenths	$\frac{9}{10}$
0.10	$\frac{10}{100}$	1.0
twenty hundredths	0.20	ten hundredths
$\frac{40}{100}$	thirty hundredths	$\frac{30}{100}$

Decimal Days Game Cards

0.40	forty hundredths	$\frac{50}{100}$	0.50
fifty hundredths	$\frac{60}{100}$	0.60	sixty hundredths
$\frac{70}{100}$	0.70	seventy hundredths	$\frac{80}{100}$
0.80	eighty hundredths	$\frac{90}{100}$	0.90
ninety hundredths	$\frac{100}{100}$	1.00	one hundred hundredths

PUT THE DOT ON THE SPOT

Objective

Students will compare and order decimals on a number line.

Anticipatory Set

Draw a large horizontal number line on the board from 0 to 1.0. Mark off every tenth, and label the number line "0," "0.1," "0.2," and so on, up to "1.0." Below the number line, draw a rectangle of the same length. Divide the rectangle into 10 equal parts that correspond with the points on the number line.

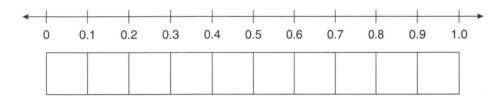

Invite students to look at the number line. Count by tenths together in unison from 0 to 1. Point to the number line as you count, moving your hand from left to right. This movement helps demonstrate the order of decimals on a number line.

Compare the number line to the model of the rectangle. Shade in each part of the rectangle as you count from one tenth all the way up to one, moving from left to right to demonstrate that the numbers are getting larger.

Purpose

Tell students that they will be using decimals on a number line to play a game. They will learn how to compare and order decimals on a number line to help their teams earn points during the game.

Input

Students are familiar with number lines that show whole numbers. Point out that whole numbers go in order from smallest to largest, moving from left to right. Inform students that decimals also have an order on the number line: "A number line with decimals also has the smallest number on the left and the largest number on the right. When comparing numbers, such as decimals on a number line, the smallest number has the least value, and the largest number has the greatest value."

Modeling

In this activity, volunteers will place a sticky note with a large dot on it on the board to locate a number on the number line. Make sure to have plenty of dot sticky notes available. Model several examples with students.

Draw students' attention back to the number line on the board. Write the decimal 0.6 on the board next to the number line. Locate that number on the number line, and place the sticky note with the dot over its spot. Say, "I put the dot on the spot!"

Then remove the sticky note, and invite a volunteer to find a different number on the number line. Invite that student to "put the dot on the spot." After several examples using this number line, erase it, and draw a new number line showing the decimals 2.5 to 4.5.

Next to the number line, write four numbers on the board in random order, such as 3.2, 4.4, 2.9, and 3.8. Invite four volunteers, one at a time, to locate these numbers using sticky notes: "Can you locate the number on the number line? Put the dot on the spot!"

Then compare the order of these decimals on the number line. Invite students to name which decimal is the least and which decimal is the greatest.

Checking for Understanding

Invite each volunteer to explain his or her strategy for locating the number on the number line. Place dots over four new numbers on the number line. Name one of the marked numbers, and ask if it is the least. Name one of the other marked numbers, and ask if it is the greatest. Have students show thumbs-up or thumbs-down to check their understanding. Continue to model examples as needed.

Guided Practice

Take the class outside to the playground blacktop. Use chalk to draw a number line from 0 to 5 or from 5 to 10. Mark the number line in tenths, spaced far enough apart to give students enough room to stand on each number. (If playing this game indoors, use masking tape to make the number line. Check that the tape can be removed easily without damaging the carpet or the floor. Mark numbers on the number line by taping numbered paper squares to the floor.)

Prepare a set of index cards to use for the game. Number the cards "0," "0.1," "0.2," and so on, up to "5.0," one number per card. (Or number them to correspond to your number line.) Make at least one card per student.

How to Play the Game

Divide the class into four equal teams to play the game. Have each team stand around the number line at the opposite four corners of the playing area. Shuffle the cards, and distribute them randomly so each student gets one card. Set aside any extra cards. (Any leftover students can be scorekeepers.)

Model how to play the first round of the game. The goal is to be the team in each round with either the least or the greatest number on the number line. Allow time for each team to look at its number card. Then have teams choose a player to go first. Encourage team members to talk quietly among themselves so other teams can't hear their strategies.

At your signal, the first players from each team find their numbers on the number line and stand in those spots. After all four players are standing in order on the number line, award one point to the team with the least number and one point to the team with the greatest number in that set. Collect these players' index cards, and prepare for the second round.

Have all four teams examine their numbers and choose one player to play the next round. At your signal, these four players find their numbers and stand on the number line. Award points the same way you did in the first round.

Continue playing until every player has had a chance to stand on the number line. The winner is the team or teams that have the most points at the end of the game. If time allows, shuffle and distribute the cards, and play the game again.

Closure

Invite students to share their teams' strategies in choosing which players competed in each round. Guide the discussion to include words such as *least* and *greatest.* Then prompt students to write an acrostic in their math journals using the word *decimal.* Tell them the acrostics should describe what they learned during the game.

Independent Practice

For homework, have students complete a copy of the **Dots on Spot reproducible (page 60).** Remind them that decimals are ordered on a number line from least to greatest, identical to the way whole numbers are ordered on a number line.

Name_____   Date_____

Dots on Spot

Directions: Find the decimals on the number line. Draw the dots.

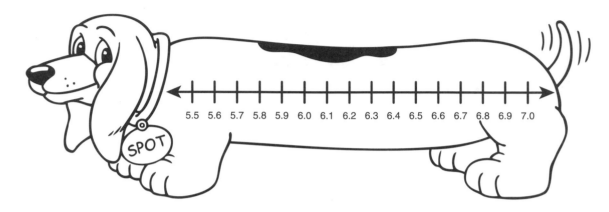

5.5 5.6 5.7 5.8 5.9 6.0 6.1 6.2 6.3 6.4 6.5 6.6 6.7 6.8 6.9 7.0

1. Find 6.2 on the number line. Draw a red dot on the spot.

2. Find 5.7 on the number line. Draw a pink dot on the spot.

3. Find 6.8 on the number line. Draw an orange dot on the spot.

4. Find 5.9 on the number line. Draw a brown dot on the spot.

5. Find 6.0 on the number line. Draw a purple dot on the spot.

6. Find 6.3 on the number line. Draw a black dot on the spot.

7. Find 5.8 on the number line. Draw a blue dot on the spot.

8. Find 6.5 on the number line. Draw a yellow dot on the spot.

9. Find 6.4 on the number line. Draw a gray dot on the spot.

10. Find 5.6 on the number line. Draw a green dot on the spot.

11. Of the numbers you marked, which is the *least*? _____

12. Of the numbers you marked, which is the *greatest*? _____

DOLLARS AND SENSE

Objective

Students will practice adding and subtracting decimals by relating the numbers to money.

Anticipatory Set

Gather several items, and attach a price tag to each one to represent a variety of decimals, such as *$8.37, $3.40,* and *$12.15.* Ask students, "If you had $20.00 and wanted to buy something, how could you know if you had enough money?" Guide the discussion toward the conclusion that one must either add until he or she reaches $20.00 or subtract starting at $20.00.

Purpose

Invite students to talk about a time they bought a favorite toy. Explain that knowing how to add and subtract decimals is very important, especially when shopping.

> The more arithmetic we can teach through declarative processes involving understanding and meaning, the more likely children will succeed in and actually enjoy mathematics.

Input

Divide the class into small groups. Give each group a set of play money to use as a model during the activity. Make sure each group has several 1-, 5-, and 10-dollar bills and several quarters, dimes, nickels, and pennies.

Write the decimals *3.8* and *5.19* on the board. Explain that 3.8 is the same as 3.80, which is equivalent to $3.80. Write "$3.80" on the board, and tell students to copy what you are writing on a piece of scrap paper. Lining up the decimal points, write "+5.19" below the first number. While completing the problem and writing the answer, tell students, "Adding decimals is the same as adding whole numbers."

Modeling

Instruct each group to use the play money to collect $3.80 and set it aside. Then have each group collect $5.19. Tell group members to work together at adding the money to check the answer.

Then model a subtraction problem on the board: 16.83 − 12.6. Point out that the decimals must line up. Remind students that 12.6 is equivalent to 12.60, which is the same as $12.60. Write the answer, and have students copy your work. Encourage them to check the answer using the paper money.

Checking for Understanding

Ask groups to demonstrate how they checked their answers with the play money. Model more examples as needed.

Guided Practice

Hold a class auction to provide more practice adding and subtracting decimals. Before holding the auction, award the class points for good behavior or turning in homework. Each point is worth $1.00 in play money. When the class has earned $20.00, hold the auction.

Invite students to bring in used or unwanted toys or other household items with their parents' permission. On the board, write a variety of prices for different kinds of items. The highest price for an item should be $20.00. Instruct students to compare the items they brought in with your examples. Then ask them to write price tags to tape onto their items. Organize the items into four groups according to price range.

Then divide the class into four groups. Each group will act as clerks to oversee the sales figures for one group of items. Give each student $20.00 in play money to spend at the auction.

Begin the auction by holding up an item. Ask if someone wants to purchase it. If only one student wants it, he or she can purchase it at the value on the price tag. Before buying it, however, the student must state how much money he or she has, subtract the item's price from that amount on a piece of paper, and then state how much money he or she has left to spend. The clerks from that group must also work the subtraction problem to check the answer. If more than one student wants a certain item, auction it off to the highest bidder. If more than one student is able to pay $20.00 for the item, put the students' names in a hat, and draw at random. Continue the auction until all items have been purchased or students have spent most of their money.

Closure

After the auction, add up the amount of money that students did not spend. Write the final amount on the board. Then ask students to respond to the following question in their math journals: "If I had that much money to spend, how would I spend it?"

Independent Practice

For homework, instruct students to refer to the work they copied from the board to write two original addition and subtraction problems using decimals. Have them solve the problems and draw a picture of cash and coins to represent the answers.

A PORTRAIT OF PARTS

Objective

Students will create and use decimal and fraction models to show parts of a whole using place value through the thousandths.

Anticipatory Set

Cut out 10 copies of the grid on the **Place Value Grid reproducible (page 24).** Stack the grids end to end, attach them to a tall sheet of butcher paper posted on the wall, and outline the whole shape to create a 10-story building. Remove the 10 grids (save them for later) before showing the high-rise to students. Write "1 High-Rise Building" next to the outline. Ask students, "What is a high-rise? How do you think we will use this picture to learn math?" Have students record their ideas in their math journals.

Purpose

Explain to students that many things around them are divided into smaller parts, such as apartment buildings and pizzas. In math, we use numbers called *decimals* and *fractions* to identify parts of a whole. In this activity, students will use decimals and fractions to identify equal parts of a high-rise building.

Input

Display the following place-value comparison for students. Remind students that our number system is based on groups of ten, with each place ten times bigger or smaller than the next. Each place increases by tens from right to left and decreases by tens from left to right.

Thousands	Hundreds	Tens	Ones
1,000	($\div$ 10) 100	($\div$ 10) 10	($\div$ 10) 1
Ones	**Tens**	**Hundreds**	**Thousands**
1	($\times$ 10) 10	($\times$ 10) 100	($\times$ 10) 1,000

Continue, explaining that our number system includes even smaller sizes than one whole by dividing one whole into equal parts, such as cutting one pan of brownies into equal-sized bars or pieces. Explain that we use special numbers called decimals or fractions to identify those parts, as shown below (extend the previous place-value comparison).

	Ones	Tenths	Hundredths	Thousandths
Decimals	1	0.1	0.01	0.001
Fractions	$\dfrac{1}{1}$	$\dfrac{1}{10}$	$\dfrac{1}{100}$	$\dfrac{1}{1,000}$

Point out that in the decimal system, a decimal point is used to indicate parts (less than 1), whereas in fractions, a line is used. Compare place value to different-sized puzzle pieces—10-piece puzzle, 100-piece puzzle, and 1,000-piece puzzle—all of which form the same whole puzzle. One tenth (0.1 or $\frac{1}{10}$) is 1 out of 10 equal parts, one hundredth (0.01 or $\frac{1}{100}$) is 1 out of 100 equal parts, and one thousandth (0.001 or $\frac{1}{1,000}$) is 1 out of 1,000 equal parts.

> Numerical representations help students develop mental models of arithmetic that connect to their intuitive number sense.

Modeling

At the bottom of the high-rise outline, attach one grid facedown (so the gridlines do not show). Ask students to predict how many grids are needed to fill the entire high-rise. Then attach all 10 grids facedown, demonstrating that each one represents $\frac{1}{10}$ of the whole high-rise. Write "$\frac{1}{10}$" next to each grid.

Then turn over the bottom grid to show the gridlines. Explain that this grid (or part of the building) is divided into 10 rows of 10 squares, or 100 squares in all. Point out that each row represents $\frac{1}{10}$ of the grid, and each small square represents $\frac{1}{100}$ of the grid. Ask students, "How much does each square represent for the entire building?"

Turn over all 10 grids to show the gridlines. Because there are 10 grids, and each grid has 100 squares, there are 1,000 squares in all. Therefore, each square represents $\frac{1}{1,000}$ of the building. Each row represents $\frac{1}{100}$ of the building.

Color one square blue, and write on the board, "$\frac{1}{1,000}$, or 0.001, of the building is blue." Color one row red, and write, "$\frac{1}{100}$, or 0.01, of the building is red." Then color two rows green. Ask students, "What fraction or decimal tells how much of the building is green?" Write "$\frac{2}{100}$, or 0.02, of the building is green."

Checking for Understanding

Alongside the 10 grids, write the ordinal numbers *1st* through *10th* from bottom to top to identify the stories of the high-rise. Then draw a brown door and two yellow windows on the bottom story. Ask students, "Which fraction (or decimal) of this 1st story contains the door?" ($\frac{10}{100}$ or $\frac{1}{10}$), "Which fraction (or decimal) contains windows?" ($\frac{18}{100}$ or $\frac{9}{50}$), and "So far, which fraction (or decimal) of the entire building contains the door and windows?" ($\frac{28}{100}$ or $\frac{7}{25}$).

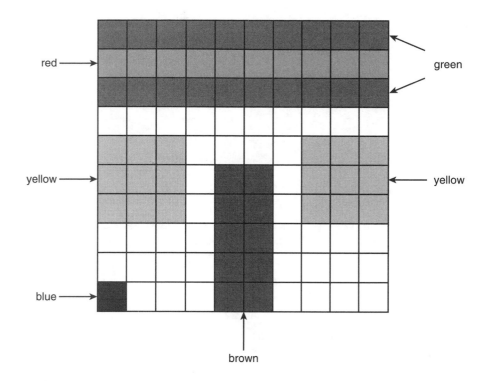

Guided Practice

Leave the bottom grid on display, and remove the remaining nine grids. Divide the class into nine groups, and give one grid to each group. Give each group 5 minutes to color its grid using the same five colors (blue, red, green, yellow, brown). Encourage them to color rows or sections of squares for each color. After students finish coloring their grids, reassemble the high-rise. Then work with students to write sentences that demonstrate which fraction or decimal of the story or the whole building is represented by each color.

Closure

Ask students, "Why is it important to know about fractions and decimals?" Have them write in their journals what they learned about fractions and decimals and explain how that information can help them in everyday life.

Independent Practice

For homework, invite students to color their own hundreds grids and record which parts per hundred are represented by each color. Have them write the numbers on a separate color key, writing both the fraction and the decimal value for each color.

Extending the Activity

Extend the activity to include addition and subtraction of fractions or decimals, using the colored sections as models, for example, $1/10$ *of the first grid is red, and* $2/10$ *of the second grid is red, so* $1/10 + 2/10 = 3/10$ *red.* You might also include instruction about equivalent fractions, such as $1/100 = 10/1,000$.

GROCERY BILL MATH

Objective

Students will estimate and calculate decimal sums and differences while playing a game of speed shopping.

Anticipatory Set

In advance, have students cut out pictures of priced grocery items from print advertisements and glue them onto cardstock to make food cards. Then ask, "Suppose you have $50 to spend on food at a grocery store. How could you quickly determine whether you have enough money to buy a group of items in your grocery cart without using a calculator, pen, or pencil?"

Purpose

Explain to students that estimating sums and differences can help them quickly determine if they have enough cash to buy all the items they put in their grocery cart before getting in line to pay for them. Point out that buyers do not always have a checkbook, credit card, or debit card available to use for purchases. In this activity, students will discover how estimation can help them shop quickly and efficiently to determine how many items they can purchase with a given amount of cash.

Input

Review with students how decimals and place value are used to record money amounts. Remind them that our money system extends only to the second digit beyond the decimal point to the hundredths place. Also review how to add and subtract money, showing how to align the decimal points and regroup. Include column addition and subtraction for different amounts, for example,

Purchases	Payment
$3.45	$50.00 cash
$19.95	$49.69
$10.75	$0.31 change
$2.35	
+$13.19	
$49.69	

Remind students to use mental math strategies to help them add columns of numbers quickly, such as the commutative property to find sums of 10. Then review how to use estimation (front-end estimation, rounding, clustering, or a combination) to quickly determine the approximate amount of money needed to buy a group of items, such as those whose prices are listed above. For example, if rounding to the nearest dollar, $3 + $20 + $11 + $2 + $13 ≈ $49.

Modeling

Help students set up a mock grocery store inside or outside the classroom. Display the priced food picture cards on different walls, or place them on rows of desks set up like the aisles of a grocery store.

Explain to students that they will play a game of speed shopping in which they will take turns racing to collect priced items that total as close to a given amount of money as possible ($5, $10, $20, $50, or $100) without going over. Point out that they will need to use their estimation skills to help them speed shop.

Invite two volunteers to help demonstrate the game, giving each $50 in play money (or just announcing the target amount) and 1 minute to shop. After time is up, display the food cards each player chose. Ask the class to estimate the total amount for each player and predict the winner. Then have students calculate on paper or use a calculator to check the total and announce the winner (the player closest to $50 without going over). Explain that the winner earns that amount of money for his or her team. The team with the most money at the end of the game wins.

> Whenever you ask students to estimate a number, give them a reason for doing so. Making the task relevant, interesting, and significant invites students to care and, consequently, invites them to engage in mathematics.

Checking for Understanding

Before starting the game, ask the following questions to check for understanding: "What is the goal of this game? How are decimals used to play the game? Why do players need to know how to estimate? If you had $20, could you win by choosing items that cost $10.05 and $9.99? Why?"

Guided Practice

Divide the class into teams, and have each team take turns racing to shop for items within a specific budget ($5, $10, $20, $50, or $100) and time limit (1 minute or 30 seconds). Remind students that the player who comes closest to the target amount without going over wins that amount (the total value collected).

At the end of each round, invite the class (or an assigned checker) to add the amounts and announce the winner. List the amounts earned on a scoreboard, and put back the collected items after each round. After the game, invite the class to work together to add and check team totals to determine who won the game.

Closure

Ask students to summarize in their journals what they did in math class and how those skills can be used in everyday life. Encourage them to discuss their ideas with classmates before writing them in their journals.

Independent Practice

Read aloud or display the prices of items listed on grocery bills, at least five items per bill. Ask students to write their estimates for each bill (not including sales tax). Allow only 30 seconds for students to write each answer. Then have students exchange papers and check each other's estimates as you read aloud the answers. Award students credit for reasonable estimates, within 10% of the exact answer. Invite volunteers to explain how they estimated correctly.

Extending the Activity

- Have students calculate the acceptable range of estimates within 10% of the exact amount. First, move the decimal point one place to the left to get 10%. Then, add that amount to or subtract it from the total to get the range of estimates.
- Have students include sales tax. Show them how to convert the percentage tax to a decimal, multiply to get the total amount of tax, and then add that number to the total purchase. Or tell students to use 10% as the sales tax (slightly overestimating) and move the decimal point to determine the approximate tax. For example, 10% of $24.00 = $2.40, so $24.00 + $2.40 = $26.40.
- Include discounts in the game, such as coupons for 50¢ off the purchase price. You might also include percentage discounts, having students convert percentages to decimals and then multiply to determine the amount of the discount.
- Have students participate in the online Global Grocery List Project at http://landmark-project.com/ggl/, where they can share local grocery prices to build a growing table of data. Encourage them to use the data to write their own math problems.

PARTY PLANNERS

Objective

Students will organize and calculate the costs of different parties using whole numbers and decimals to add, subtract, multiply, divide, and complete patterns.

Anticipatory Set

Invite students to share the kinds of things they like to see and do at parties, such as games, gifts, and treats. Write "Party Planners Inc." on the board, and ask students, "What math skills do you think this company will need to plan and organize parties of different sizes?" Invite students to share their ideas as you list them on the board.

Purpose

Explain to students that people who run their own businesses must know a variety of math skills, including how to calculate using whole numbers and decimals. In this activity, students will explore math skills used by a party-planning business, calculating the cost of supplies for different-sized parties.

> Learning mathematics is easier and more meaningful when the learner can connect mathematical operations and concepts to solving problems in the real world.

Input

Show students how to complete the following problems. Point out that they will need to know all these skills for the upcoming activity. Encourage them to ask questions and copy the following examples into their math journals.

- $3.65 + $.75 + $299.00 = ? (*$303.40*)
- $2,780.50 − (20% of $2,780.50) = ? (*$2,780.50 − $556.10 = $2,224.40*)
- $75/hr × 2.5 hr = ? (*$187.50*)
- $399.00 ÷ 20 people = ? (*$19.95 per person*)
- $20.00 for 5 people, $40.00 for 10 people, $80.00 for ? (*20 people*)

Modeling

Give each student a copy of the **Party Planners Price Chart reproducible (page 71),** and display a copy to guide instruction. Explain that businesses often use charts and number patterns to help them organize and calculate different amounts. Demonstrate how to use addition, subtraction, multiplication, and division patterns to complete each row of the chart as students follow along on their own charts. Point out different ways to calculate and check answers, such as using values for 10 people or 50 people to calculate the answers for 100 people.

Invite volunteers to help fill in the missing values as you complete each row of the chart. Point out that the price for game tables is an exception to the rule; prices are based on the cost of each full table, not just the number of people at the party. For example, a party of 10 people must pay for two full game tables even though they do not need all 12 seats.

Checking for Understanding

Ask students to explain the difference between calculating party prices for items that have a flat rate and calculating prices for those that are priced per person. Then ask, "How can you use price patterns from the chart to determine the cost for 40 or 400 people?"

Guided Practice

Give each student a copy of the **Party Planners Reservation List reproducible (page 72)**. Work together to calculate prices for the Jones party. Point out that the time frame for this party (1.5 hours) does not matter for the items and services chosen. Invite students to suggest ways to calculate the cost for four seafood meals and six vegetarian meals (*e.g., cost of five meals – cost of one meal; cost of five meals + cost of one meal*). Also, guide students in calculating the 20% deposit (total × 0.20) and subtracting that number to get the remaining balance. Explain that customers often pay a deposit in advance and then pay the rest after the party.

Closure

Have students list in their math journals the math and organizational skills they used for this lesson. Ask, "What was the purpose of this lesson? What did you like about it? How might you use this knowledge in the future?"

Independent Practice

Have students complete the Party Planners Reservation List on their own or with partners. Suggest that they use the Party Planners Price Chart to write and solve their own math problems. When correcting students' work, check that they used the price chart correctly.

Name_____ Date_____

Party Planners Price Chart

Directions: Complete this chart for each party.

	Pricing	5 People	10 People	20 People	50 People	100 People
Luxury Dining Hall	$4.00 per person	$20	$40			
DJ Music	flat rate	$100/ hour	$100/hour	$100/hour	$100/hour	$100/hour
Live Band	flat rate	$200/ hour	$200/hour	$200/hour	$200/hour	$200/hour
Party Favors	$ _____ per person	$12.50		$50		
***Game Tables**	$150 per table (seats 6)					
Appetizers	$ _____ per person	$17.50				
Meat Meal	$ _____ per person			$399		
Poultry Meal	$ _____ per person	$60				
Seafood Meal	$ _____ per person			$315		
Vegetarian Meal	$ _____ per person				$500	
Buffet Meal	$ _____ per person		$225			
Dessert Bar	$ _____ per person					$750
Special Drinks	$ _____ per person			$90		
Photographer	flat rate	$75/hour + $1.50/ photo	$75/hour + 1.50/photo	$75/hour + $1.50/ photo	$75/hour + $1.50/ photo	$75/hour + $1.50/ photo

Must pay for the entire game table.

71

Party Planners Reservation List

Directions: Use the Party Planners Price Chart to complete the list for each party.

Jones Party
(20 people, 1.5 hours)

	Price
Luxury Dining Hall	
5 Meat Meals	
5 Poultry Meals	
4 Seafood Meals	
6 Vegetarian Meals	
Dessert Bar	
Special Drinks	
TOTAL	
20% Deposit	
Remaining Balance	

Phan Party
(50 people, 2 hours)

	Price
DJ Music	
Party Favors	
Appetizers	
Buffet Meals	
Dessert Bar	
Photographer	
+ 36 Photos	
TOTAL	
20% Deposit	
Remaining Balance	

Dominguez Party
(100 people, 2 hours)

	Price
Live Band	
Game Tables	
Appetizers	
Buffet Meals	
Dessert Bar	
Special Drinks	
Photographer	
+ 72 Photos	
TOTAL	
20% Deposit	
Remaining Balance	

Harris Party
(400 people, 4 hours)

	Price
Luxury Dining	
DJ Music	
Party Favors	
Buffet Meals	
Dessert Bar	
Special Drinks	
Photographer	
+ 144 Photos	
TOTAL	
20% Deposit	
Remaining Balance	

FRACTION COOKING

Objective

Students will discover how addition, subtraction, multiplication, and division of fractions are used in cooking.

Anticipatory Set

Display a carton of a dozen eggs, some clear glass or plastic bowls, and a clear measuring cup with fraction labels. Say to students, "Chefs and cooks need good math skills to prepare recipes. How do you think math is used in cooking?" List students' suggestions on the board.

Purpose

Explain to students that math is used in almost every aspect of cooking, including determining the quantity of different items, accurately measuring amounts using kitchen tools, and calculating the cost of ingredients. In this activity, students will use fractions and other math skills to calculate the ingredients used in a recipe.

Input

Ask students to write the following definitions and examples in their math journals. Tell them that they will use this information for the upcoming activity. Encourage them to ask questions and share examples for each definition.

- **Fraction:** Method for writing a number less than 1; represents equal parts of a whole.
- **Numerator:** Top number in a fraction; tells how much of the whole is used.
- **Denominator:** Bottom number in a fraction; tells how many parts make up the whole.
- **Common (like) denominators:** Fractions that have the same denominator.
- **Uncommon (unlike) denominators:** Fractions that have different denominators.
- **Improper fraction:** Fraction whose numerator is larger than its denominator.
- **Mixed number:** Whole number and a fractional amount.
- **Equivalent fractions:** Fractions that represent the same amount.

Fraction	Equivalent Fraction	Fraction Model
$\dfrac{3 \text{ numerator}}{6 \text{ denominator}}$	$\dfrac{1}{2}$	

Fraction	Equivalent Fraction	Fraction Model
$\dfrac{7}{6}$	$1\dfrac{1}{6}$	

Modeling

Display a carton of 12 eggs. Select 1 of the eggs. Ask students, "Which fraction is 1 egg out of this whole carton of eggs?" Write on the board, "1 out of 12 eggs, or $^1/_{12}$ of the carton."

Place one egg in a clear bowl and five more eggs in another bowl. Ask students, "Which fraction is in this first bowl?" ($^1/_{12}$). "In the second bowl?" ($^5/_{12}$). Place all six eggs in the same bowl. Then ask, "Which number sentence can I write to show what I just did?" Write, "$^1/_{12} + ^5/_{12} = ^6/_{12}$ of the carton." Point out that the addends $^1/_{12}$ and $^5/_{12}$ have the same (like) denominators. You added only the numerators to get the sum $^6/_{12}$; the denominator stayed the same. Remind students that the denominator tells how many equal parts complete the whole, which does not change.

Then ask, "Which number sentence can I write to show which fraction of the carton of eggs is left?" Write "$^{12}/_{12} - ^6/_{12} = ^6/_{12}$ left." Point out that $^{12}/_{12}$ (12 out of 12) is a fractional way of writing "one whole" or "one carton of eggs." Any time the numerator and the denominator are the same, the fraction equals one whole. Ask, "Why did I use $^{12}/_{12}$ instead of 1?" (*You need a common denominator of 12.*). Point out that you must have a common denominator to add or subtract fractions.

Explain that 6 eggs are half of 12 eggs. Write "$^6/_{12} = ^1/_2$." Explain that $^6/_{12}$ and $^1/_2$ are called *equivalent fractions*—they represent the same amount. When you add or subtract fractions that do not have the same denominator, you must use equivalent fractions that have a common denominator. In other words, write "$^{12}/_{12} - ^6/_{12}$" instead of "$^{12}/_{12} - ^1/_2$."

Write the following fractions, pointing out that they all are equivalent (equal) to $^1/_2$ and that each numerator is half of its denominator: "$^1/_2 = ^6/_{12}, \ ^{12}/_{24}, \ ^{18}/_{36}$" (*$^1/_2$ of one carton of eggs, $^1/_2$ of two cartons of eggs, $^1/_2$ of three cartons of eggs*). Then demonstrate that when you multiply (or divide) both the numerator and the denominator by the same number, you get an equivalent fraction:

Use concrete manipulatives whenever possible. This helps students develop visual and spatial representations of the concept or skill being taught.

$\dfrac{1(\times 6)}{2(\times 6)} = \dfrac{6}{12}$	$\dfrac{1(\times 12)}{2(\times 12)} = \dfrac{12}{24}$	$\dfrac{1(\times 18)}{2(\times 18)} = \dfrac{18}{36}$
$\dfrac{6(\div 6)}{12(\div 6)} = \dfrac{1}{2}$	$\dfrac{12(\div 12)}{24(\div 12)} = \dfrac{1}{2}$	$\dfrac{18(\div 18)}{36(\div 18)} = \dfrac{1}{2}$

Checking for Understanding

Write the following three examples on the board. Ask students to identify the correct example and explain why the other two are incorrect (*The third example is correct. The first example is incorrect because the denominators are not the same; you do not subtract denominators. The second example is incorrect because the denominators were added together.*).

$$\frac{12}{12} - \frac{1}{3} = \frac{11}{9}$$

$$\frac{12}{12} - \frac{1}{3} = \frac{12}{12} - \frac{4}{12} = \frac{8}{24}$$

$$\frac{12}{12} - \frac{1}{3} = \frac{12}{12} - \frac{4}{12} = \frac{8}{12}$$

Guided Practice

Give students a copy of the **Fraction Cooking reproducible (page 76).** Point out that the muffin recipe yields one dozen muffins, just like the number of eggs. Show students how to use addition, subtraction, and mixed numbers to fill in the missing numbers for two dozen muffins (double the amount), including how to change improper fractions to mixed numbers.

Independent Practice

Have students compete the Fraction Cooking reproducible, filling in the numbers for three dozen muffins and answering the questions. Encourage student pairs to check and compare answers.

Closure

Invite students to help make the muffins, measuring and mixing together the ingredients for a hands-on experience. Bake the muffins later, and distribute them for students to enjoy. Invite students to write in their math journals about how knowing how to add and subtract fractions might help them in other areas of their lives.

Name_____   Date_____

Fraction Cooking

Directions: Complete the recipe chart. Then answer the questions below.

Carrot Walnut Muffins

1 Dozen Muffins	2 Dozen Muffins	3 Dozen Muffins
$1\frac{3}{4}$ cups wheat flour	$1\frac{3}{4} + 1\frac{3}{4} = 3\frac{1}{2}$ cups	
$\frac{1}{2}$ cup brown sugar	$\frac{1}{2} + \frac{1}{2} = 1$ cup	
1 tsp. baking powder		
$\frac{3}{4}$ cup skim milk		
1 egg (lightly beaten)		
3 Tbs. butter		
$1\frac{1}{8}$ cup grated carrots		
$\frac{1}{3}$ cup chopped walnuts		
$\frac{1}{2}$ tsp. cinnamon		

Cooking Directions: Preheat oven to 400° F. Combine flour, sugar, and baking powder in a bowl. Stir in milk and egg. Then mix in butter. Stir in grated carrots, walnuts, and cinnamon. Spoon mixture equally into 12 greased muffin tins. Bake for 20 to 25 minutes.

1. If you make 3 dozen muffins, what fraction of a dozen eggs will you have left? _____

2. If you sell 9 out of 3 dozen muffins, what fraction will you have sold?_____

3. If you want to figure out how much of each ingredient you need for 4 dozen muffins, how can you use the amounts calculated for 2 dozen muffins?

_____

Write Your Own Problem

On the back of this paper, write and solve your own math problem about fractions and cooking. Use information from the muffin recipe, or use a recipe of your own.

CALLING ALL CONSTRUCTION WORKERS

Objective

Students will work in cooperative groups to add, subtract, multiply, and divide fractions and decimals as they plan and draw floor plans for a community project.

Anticipatory Set

Invite students to share what they know about Habitat for Humanity and other organizations that build and repair homes for people in need. Ask, "How do you think math is used for that kind of work?" Invite students to share their ideas.

Purpose

Explain that there are organizations, such as Habitat for Humanity, that build homes internationally for families in need. Dedicated, caring volunteers perform all of the construction to help others. In this activity, students will work in teams to plan homes for a Homes for Humanity project.

> Whenever a teacher attaches a positive emotion to the mathematics lesson, it not only gets attention but also helps students to see mathematics as having real-life applications.

Input

Review the following math skills with students. Show them how to solve each example while students follow along in their math journals. You might also have them confirm your calculations using calculators.

Add and Subtract Fractions and Mixed Numbers

Rules: Use a common denominator, regroup if needed to add or subtract, and write the final answer as a proper fraction or mixed number in lowest terms.

Example: $2\frac{1}{3} - 1\frac{3}{4} = 2\frac{4}{12} - 1\frac{9}{12} = 1\frac{5}{12}$

Multiply and Divide Fractions and Mixed Numbers

Rules: Change mixed numbers to improper fractions, change division to multiplication by using the inverse for the second term, cross-simplify before multiplying, and write the final answer in lowest terms.

Example: $2\frac{1}{3} \div 1\frac{3}{4} = \frac{7}{3} \div \frac{7}{4} = \frac{7}{3} \times \frac{4}{7} = \frac{4}{3}$ or $1\frac{1}{3}$

Calculate Perimeter
(Distance Around) and Area (Space Inside)

Rules: The perimeter of any polygon = the sum of the lengths of its sides. Area of rectangle or square = length × width. Area of triangle = $\frac{1}{2}$ (base × height).

Perimeter Example: Perimeter of rectangle with length of 12½ ft (3.81 m) and width of 8 ft (2.44 m) = 12½ ft + 8 ft + 12½ ft + 8 ft = 41 ft (3.81 m + 2.44 m + 3.81 m + 2.44 m = 12.5 m).

Area Example: Area of rectangle = 12½ ft × 8 ft = 100 ft² (3.81 m × 2.44 m = 9.3 m²).

Add, Subtract, Multiply, and Divide Decimals

Rules: For addition and subtraction, stack and align the decimals, and use zeros as placeholders before calculating. Bring down the aligned decimal to place in the final answer. For multiplication and division, calculate decimals like whole numbers, and place the decimal in the correct position. Count the total place value positions for all multiplication factors, or place the decimal directly upward in the answer of a long division problem (when the dividend is the decimal).

Addition Example: 6.2 m + 0.78 m + 11 m = 6.20 m + 0.78 m + 11.00 m = 17.98 m

Multiplication Example: 6.2 m × 0.78 m × 11 m = 53.196 m = 53.20 m (Multiply, place the decimal three positions from the end of the product, and round off accordingly.)

Modeling

Explain to students that they will work in teams to draw a house floor plan for a family in need. Each team will decide on its own layout, and team members must include labeled dimensions in both customary and metric units.

Show examples of floor plans, such as those downloaded from the Internet or flyers and printed brochures from real estate agencies and home construction stores. Point out the features of each floor plan, including labeled dimensions, scale conversion, and various room shapes.

Use a large sheet of grid paper or an overhead transparency to demonstrate how to draw and calculate the area of an irregular-shaped room (such as an L-shaped room). First, divide the room into regular-shaped sections (such as two rectangles). Then, find the area of each section. Finally, add those products to get the total area. Show both customary and metric units (including both fractions and decimals), and demonstrate how to convert from one to the other using 1 ft ≈ 0.30 m. Describe how to use a key scale, such as 1 grid square = 1 ft, to draw each length.

Guided Practice

Guide students as they organize their floor plans. Direct them to include the following building requirements:

- a total area (floor area) of 1,400 to 1,800 ft² (426.72 to 548.64 m²), at least three bedrooms (minimum size 8 × 10 ft or 2.44 × 3.05 m), one living room, one dining room, one kitchen, two bathrooms, an entry hall, and a backyard that is 800 to 1,000 ft^2 (243.84 to 304.8 m^2);

- mixed numbers for some of the dimensions, such as 12¼ ft;
- at least one irregular-shaped, such as L-shaped or H-shaped, room;
- a master bedroom that is 1½ times the area of the smallest bedroom;
- a master bathroom that is ¼ the area of the master bedroom;
- another bathroom that is ¾ the area of the master bathroom; and
- a living room that is 2 times the area of the dining room.

Tell students to begin by making an organized list of all the rooms they plan to include in their houses, listing the estimated area of each room to get a total area of 1,400 to 1,800 ft^2 (426.72 to 548.64 m^2). Show them an example using the dimensions of your classroom as a reference. You might permit them to use calculators.

Then have students draw rough sketches of their floor plans to get a general idea of the layout before they draw their final versions. Show an example on the board of a connected master bedroom and bathroom, pointing out that the rooms may be drawn in different shapes to get the same square footage (e.g., an 8 × 4 ft room and a 6 × 6 ft room have the same area).

Monitor students' progress as they work. You might encourage them to research floor plans on the Internet or use computer software to design their plans.

Checking for Understanding

Ask volunteers to describe how they will complete the assignment step by step. Ask questions such as, *What details must you include in your floor plan? How will you use your list and sketch to help you draw it?* and *How will your team share responsibilities and check each other's work?*

Independent Practice

Have each team make a poster that shows its final floor plan and includes a written summary telling why their plan should be used to build a home. Encourage teams to include pictures and other artistic elements on their posters. Allow several days for students to complete the assignment.

Closure

Invite each team to share its results, displaying and describing the floor plan and reading aloud the descriptive summary. Encourage students to describe how their teams organized ideas and worked together to complete the project. Ask classmates to critique each other's work and tell what they liked about each floor plan. Ask students to write in their math journals about their favorite floor plans and list reasons to support their opinions.

3

Geometry and Measurement

81

DETECTIVE ANGLE

Objective

Students will use simple tools to identify and classify angles.

Anticipatory Set

Novelty and motivation are both linked to increased retention rates.

Appeal to students' sense of excitement by talking to them as if they were detectives ready to find and explore clues. Explain that you are going to tell them top-secret information about how to use something as ordinary as a piece of paper to search for clues.

Purpose

Tell students that they are on a secret mission to find the right angles. The number one top-secret tool they will use to crack the case will be disguised as an ordinary piece of paper. This way, no one will suspect that they are on a secret mission.

Input

Explain that before detectives go in search of clues, they have to get the facts. Using the **What's Your Angle? reproducible (page 86)** as a guide, draw $\angle$HQV on the board. Say, "An angle that forms a square corner is a *right angle.*" Write the term on the board. Then write the name of the angle three ways: "$\angle$Q, $\angle$HQV, $\angle$VQH." Draw several more examples of right angles. Write the name of each angle three ways.

Draw $\angle$DFL on the board. Tell students, "An angle that is less than a right angle is called an *acute angle.* To remember this term, think of it as a much smaller, 'cute' angle. It is 'a cute,' or an acute, angle." Write the term on the board. Write the name of the angle three ways. Draw several more examples of acute angles, and write the name of each angle three ways.

Then draw $\angle$PWJ on the board. Tell students, "An angle that is greater than a right angle is called an *obtuse angle.* Say *obtuse,* and open your mouth wide. This angle looks like a big, wide-open mouth." Write the term on the board. Write the name of the angle three ways. Draw several more examples of obtuse angles, and write the name of each angle three ways.

Modeling

Inform students that now that they know the facts, they are ready to start searching for clues. Their mission is to find objects in the classroom with right angles. Name several objects with right angles, such as a book, a window, and a desk. Don't name too many, because soon students will be on a mission to look for objects in the classroom.

Checking for Understanding

Check to make sure students understand how to identify a right angle. Point out an object with a right angle, and ask students to show thumbs-up for yes and thumbs-down for no. Model more angles on the board as needed.

Guided Practice

Give each student a copy of the **Detective Angle reproducible (pages 84–85).** Read the story aloud as students follow along. When finished, tell students that their top-secret tool to help them find clues is a handy dandy Right Angle Tool. Disguised as an ordinary piece of paper, it can help them measure an angle to check whether it is an acute, an obtuse, or a right angle. If an angle matches a corner of the paper, it is a right angle.

Send students in pairs on their top-secret mission—to find as many right angles in the classroom as possible. Instruct them to use their Detective Angle reproducibles as their Right Angle Tools during their search. Direct them to list as many right angles as they can find.

Closure

After students are finished, invite them to share their lists. Praise everyone for a job well done. Have students draw pictures in their math journals of an acute angle, an obtuse angle, and a right angle. Prompt them to write about the strategies they used to find right angles in the classroom.

Independent Practice

Have students complete a copy of the What's Your Angle reproducible for homework. Remind them of the three ways to write the name of an angle.

Detective Angle

right angle

acute angle

obtuse angle

My name is Detective Angle. I always solve the case! How do I do it? Easy! I just look for the right angle. Take, for example, the case I had this morning. My neighbor, Snooks, ran over to my house. His cat, Harriet, ran behind him.

"Help!" shouted Snooks.

"Meow!" cried Harriet.

"What's the angle?" I asked.

Snooks explained the situation. "My aunt ran out of cat food, so she took Harriet's! Harriet is really hungry. But my aunt left me a note. Read it!" Snooks shoved the note in my face. I got out my magnifying glass and read the note: *Sorry! I took all the cat food, but I hid one can where you would be sure to find it. Here is the clue: Look for something with four right angles that sits on a shelf. It is Harriet's favorite.*

I looked at Snooks. "Why did your aunt hide the cat food from Harriet?"

"Harriet knows how to use the can opener," Snooks said.

"Meow!" cried Harriet.

"Strange cat," I said. "But I can solve this case. I'll just look for the right angle!"

First, I grabbed my handy dandy Right Angle Tool. Then we ran over to Snooks's house. First thing I did was look for a shelf. There was a bookshelf next to the couch. I pulled off a book. I used my Right Angle Tool to measure the angles of all four corners.

"Bingo!" I cried. "A book has four right angles!"

"How do you know?" asked Snooks.

"Because I'm using my handy dandy Right Angle Tool," I explained.

"But you're just using a sheet of paper," Snooks said.

Detective Angle (Continued)

"That's right," I replied. "Any rectangular sheet of paper will do. Every corner on a rectangular sheet of paper is a right angle. I just hold it up to the angle I am looking at and compare it. If the angle is smaller than the corner of the paper, I know it is an **acute angle.** If the angle is bigger than the corner of the paper, I know it is an **obtuse angle.** But if the angle matches the corner of the paper, I know it is a **right angle.**"

I tapped on the book I had just measured. "A book has four right angles!" I opened the book. "But there is no cat food inside."

"How could a can of cat food be inside of a book?" Snooks asked.

Somehow his question gave me an idea. I looked at all the books on the shelf. One book looked different than the others. This book was made of wood. I pulled out *The Cricket in Times Square* by George Selden. On the front was a picture of a cat.

"That is Harriet's favorite book," Snooks said.

"Harriet can read?" I asked.

"No, of course not," Snooks said. "Cats can't read. She likes to look at the pictures."

I opened the book. It wasn't a book at all! It was a wooden box designed to look like a book. Inside was a can of cat food. "Case solved!" I shouted in triumph.

"Meow!" cried Harriet. She ran out of the room.

"Where is Harriet going?" I asked.

"She went to get the can opener," Snooks replied.

"Strange cat," I said. I folded up my handy dandy Right Angle Tool and put it in my pocket. I wanted to be ready for my next case. I knew I would solve it. I always do! I just look for the right angle.

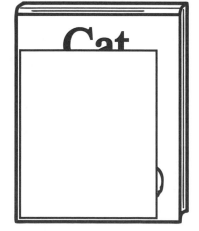

Name_____ **Date**_____

What's Your Angle?

Directions: Name each angle in three different ways. The first one is done for you. Then trace each acute angle in yellow. Trace each obtuse angle in blue. Trace each right angle in red.

1. 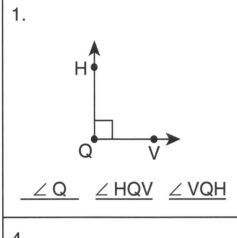 $\angle$ Q $\angle$ HQV $\angle$ VQH	2. 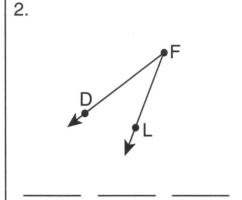 ___ ___ ___	3. 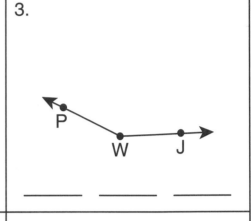 ___ ___ ___
4. 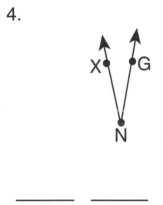 ___ ___ ___	5. 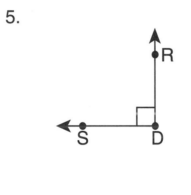 ___ ___ ___	6. 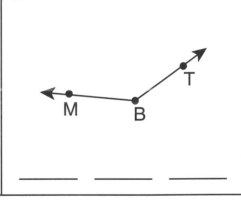 ___ ___ ___

Directions: Use your handy dandy Right Angle Tool to find eight objects that have a right angle. Name the objects.

1._____   2._____

3._____   4._____

5._____   6._____

7._____   8._____

TRICKY TRIANGLES

Objective

Students will play a card game to practice identifying and classifying triangles.

Anticipatory Set

Place a transparency of the **Tres Triangles Game Cards reproducible (page 89)** on the overhead. Tell students, "Triangles can be tricky, but today we will learn fun tricks to help us identify them and tell them apart."

Purpose

Explain that there are various kinds of triangles, but they can be classified in two ways. Tell students they will be learning a clever trick that can help them classify triangles using their handy dandy Right Angle Tools.

Input

Cover the bottom three rows of triangles on the Tres Triangles Game Cards reproducible so that only the top row is showing on the overhead. Say, "We can classify triangles by their angles." Point to the right triangle, and read aloud the definition.

Ask students, "How can we check that this triangle is a right triangle? We can use our handy dandy Right Angle Tool." Place the corner of a piece of paper in the corner of the triangle to demonstrate that it has a right angle. Repeat this process with the acute triangle and the obtuse triangle.

Modeling

Cover the top three rows of triangles on the reproducible so that only the bottom row is showing on the overhead. Tell students, "We can also classify triangles by the lengths of their sides." Point to the equilateral triangle, and read the definition aloud.

Ask students, "How can we check that all three sides on this triangle are the same length? Our handy dandy Right Angle Tool is even handier than we thought! We can also use it to measure the lengths of the sides of triangles." Measure one side of the triangle with an edge of the paper and mark the length on the paper's edge. Compare this length to the other two sides to determine that all three sides are equal. Repeat this process with the isosceles triangle and the scalene triangle.

Draw a right triangle on the board, and then invite several volunteers to draw right triangles next to yours. Encourage them to refer to the overhead and use their handy dandy Right Angle Tools as they work. Invite more students to draw models of each kind of triangle, following your lead. Take time to identify and classify each one.

Checking for Understanding

Play a simple riddle game with students to check that they understand how to identify and classify triangles. Give clues for each triangle, for example, "This triangle has two sides of equal length. What is it?" Prompt students to whisper their answers to their neighbors. Then ask a volunteer to identify the triangle (*isosceles triangle*). Draw the triangle on the board. Continue to play the riddle game, and model more examples as needed.

Guided Practice

Divide the class into teams of six players. Copy and cut out the cards from the Tres Triangles Game Cards reproducible. Each group will need four matching sets of 6 cards for a total of 24 cards. (You may wish to glue the cards to index cards or laminate them for durability.)

How to Play the Game

This card game is played similarly to the game Pig (sometimes called Spoons). Play a round of the game with a volunteer to model for the class. First, one player shuffles and distributes all the cards. Each player simultaneously discards one card from his or her hand to the player on the left. He or she then picks up the card from the player on the right.

The goal is to be the first player to collect four matching cards. When a player has four matching cards, he or she quietly touches a finger to the tip of his or her nose. As soon as one player touches his or her nose, all the other players should follow. The last player to touch his or her nose loses the round.

Players get four chances to lose a round. Each time they lose, they collect a new letter to spell out T-R-E-S. (*Tres* means "three" in Spanish.) The game is over when one player collects enough letters to spell *tres*. The other five players win.

Closure

Review the names of the different triangles and how to classify them. Prompt students to draw a picture of each of the six types of triangles in their math journals and write at least one sentence describing each one. Ask students to answer the following question, "Can a right triangle also be an isosceles triangle? Explain your answer."

Independent Practice

Have students complete a copy of the **Triangle Trickster reproducible (page 90)** for homework.

Tres Triangles Game Cards

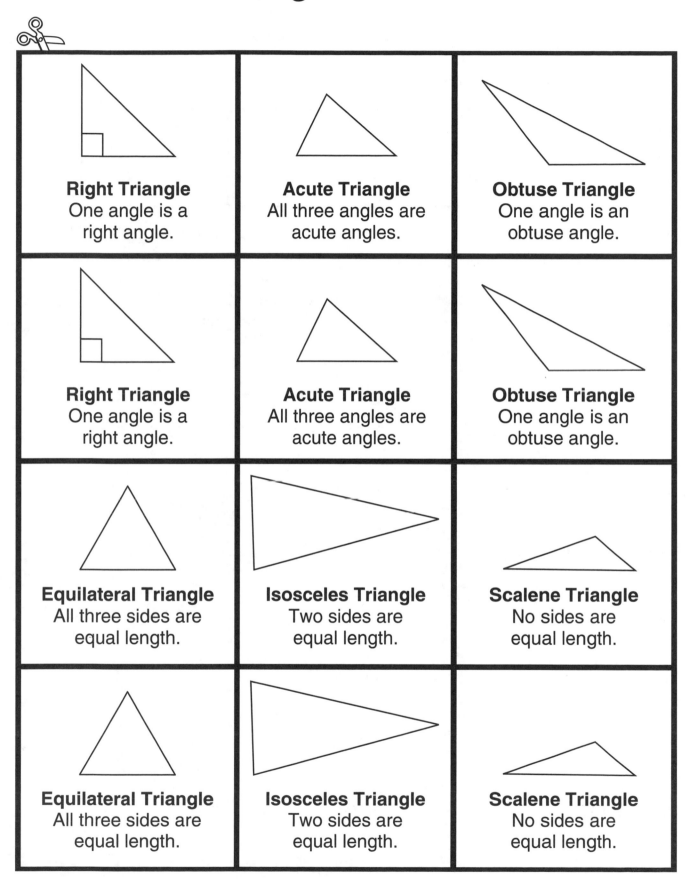

Right Triangle
One angle is a
right angle.

Acute Triangle
All three angles are
acute angles.

Obtuse Triangle
One angle is an
obtuse angle.

Right Triangle
One angle is a
right angle.

Acute Triangle
All three angles are
acute angles.

Obtuse Triangle
One angle is an
obtuse angle.

Equilateral Triangle
All three sides are
equal length.

Isosceles Triangle
Two sides are
equal length.

Scalene Triangle
No sides are
equal length.

Equilateral Triangle
All three sides are
equal length.

Isosceles Triangle
Two sides are
equal length.

Scalene Triangle
No sides are
equal length.

Name_____   Date_____

Triangle Trickster

Directions: Draw an example of each type of triangle.

1. Equilateral triangle	2. Isosceles triangle	3. Scalene triangle

Directions: Fill in the blanks with the correct answers. To solve the riddle, write the letter that matches each number below.

1. A(n) ___ ___ ___ ___ ___ triangle has a right angle.
      1   2

2. In a(n) ___ ___ ___ ___ ___ triangle, all three angles are acute angles.
         3   4

3. In a(n) ___ ___ ___ ___ ___ ___ triangle, one angle is an obtuse angle.
         5   6

4. This birthday ___ ___ ___ ___ ___ hat
         7

   is an isosceles ___ ___ ___ ___ ___ ___ ___ ___.
         8

5. This traffic sign is a(n) ___ ___ ___ ___ ___ ___ ___ ___ ___ triangle.
         9   10   11

6. No ___ ___ ___ ___ ___ are the same length
      12

   in a(n) ___ ___ ___ ___ ___ ___ ___ triangle.
            13   14

Riddle: What weighs 8,000 pounds and wears glass slippers?

___ ___ ___ ___ ___ ___ ___ ___ ___ ___ ___ ___ ___ ___
 3   9   14 12   4   1   6   13 10   7   2   11   8   5

SILLY SYMMETRY

Objective

Students will work with paper folding activities to explore examples of symmetry.

Anticipatory Set

Provide each student with a piece of white construction paper. Instruct students to fold their papers in half lengthwise. Have them write their full names in cursive along the fold. (Students with *y*'s, *g*'s, or similar letters in their names will need to loop the letters underneath and to the side to fit them above the fold. See the illustration.) Tell students to cut out their names, closely following the curves. Instruct them not to cut along the fold.

Invite each student to open up the paper with his or her name on it and glue it to a sheet of colored construction paper. Allow students time to share their artwork. Ask them to describe the shapes and designs that they see. Guide the discussion to include words such as *mirror image, matching shapes,* and *reflection.*

Purpose

Explain that identifying geometric figures that can be folded to make a mirror image is an important math concept. For this activity, students will be folding paper models to help determine which geometric figures have two matching sides.

Input

Tell students that they will be learning two new vocabulary words. Say, "An object is *symmetrical* if it can be folded in half and has two matching sides. The fold line is called the *line of symmetry.*" Explain that many objects found in nature are symmetrical. Show several pictures of symmetrical objects as you continue: "A butterfly is symmetrical. Many animals are considered symmetrical if an imaginary line is drawn down the middle. A human being is considered symmetrical. Many geometric figures are also symmetrical."

> Keep the number of items in a lesson objective within the capacity limits of working memory, and students are likely to remember more of what you presented. Less is more!

Modeling

Provide blank sheets of 8 ½ × 11 in (216 × 279 mm) paper for students to fold to explore models of symmetry. Draw a rectangle on the board. Fold a paper in half lengthwise and open it up. Tell students, "A rectangle has a line of symmetry because it can be folded in half and has two matching parts." Prompt students to fold their papers in half.

Then fold the paper in half widthwise. Prompt students to fold their papers. Say, "Some figures have more than one line of symmetry." Next, fold your paper corner to corner. Point out that this fold is not a line of symmetry because it does not form two matching halves.

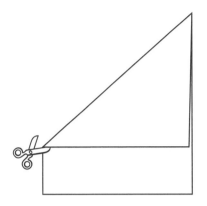

Repeat this procedure with other shapes. First, have students cut their papers into large squares by folding down one corner and cutting across the bottom, as shown.

Then ask students to fold their squares in different ways to determine the number of lines of symmetry for a square (*four*). Allow them to share their strategies for discovering this answer. Repeat this process by having students cut along a fold line to make a triangle. Invite them to discover and share the number of lines of symmetry for a triangle (*three*).

Checking for Understanding

Draw various examples of geometric figures on the board, some with lines of symmetry and some without (e.g., circle, diamond, parallelogram, pentagon). Draw a dashed line down the middle of each shape, and ask if it is a line of symmetry. Invite students to show a thumbs-up for yes or a thumbs-down for no.

Guided Practice

Give students copies of the **Silly Symmetry Snatcher reproducibles (pages 93–94).** Examine each figure together before making the snatcher. Discuss the figures in the four corners first to identify those with varying numbers of lines of symmetry. Point out each figure around the edge of the square, and ask students, "Is this a line of symmetry?" Invite them to explain their strategies for determining their answers.

Tell students to cut out the square. Guide them through the instructions for how to make the snatcher. Allow time for students to play the game several times with partners.

Closure

Invite volunteers to explain the definition of *symmetry*. Ask students to draw in their math journals an example of a geometric figure with one or more lines of symmetry.

Independent Practice

For homework, have students take their Silly Symmetry Snatchers home to play with a family member. Instruct them to make paper models of each figure on the snatcher that has a line of symmetry. Have them bring the models back to class to share.

Silly Symmetry Snatcher

How to Make the Snatcher

1. Cut out the square on page 94. Place the square facedown.	
2. Fold the square in half on the first line of symmetry. Unfold.	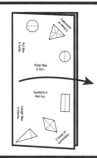
3. Repeat folding the square on the remaining three lines of symmetry. Unfold.	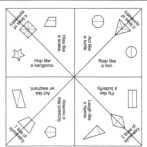
4. Place the square facedown. Bring in the four corners to the center and fold.	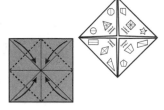
5. Turn over the square. Bring in the four corners to the center and fold.	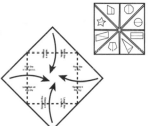
6. Insert your thumb and pointer finger of both hands into the four flaps to help the snatcher take shape.	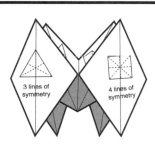

How to Play the Game

1. Player 1 holds the snatcher closed and asks Player 2 to choose one figure on the outside.

2. Player 1 opens and closes the snatcher the same number as the number of lines of symmetry for that figure.

3. Player 1 then chooses one figure showing inside the snatcher and asks, "Is this a line of symmetry?"

4. After hearing Player 2's answer, Player 1 "spells out" whether the answer was correct or incorrect by opening and closing the snatcher: Y-E-S, three times; N-O, two times.

5. If Player 2 is correct, he or she gets a turn with the snatcher. If Player 2 is incorrect, Player 1 opens the flap under the figure, and Player 2 must follow the directions inside.

Silly Symmetry Snatcher (Continued)

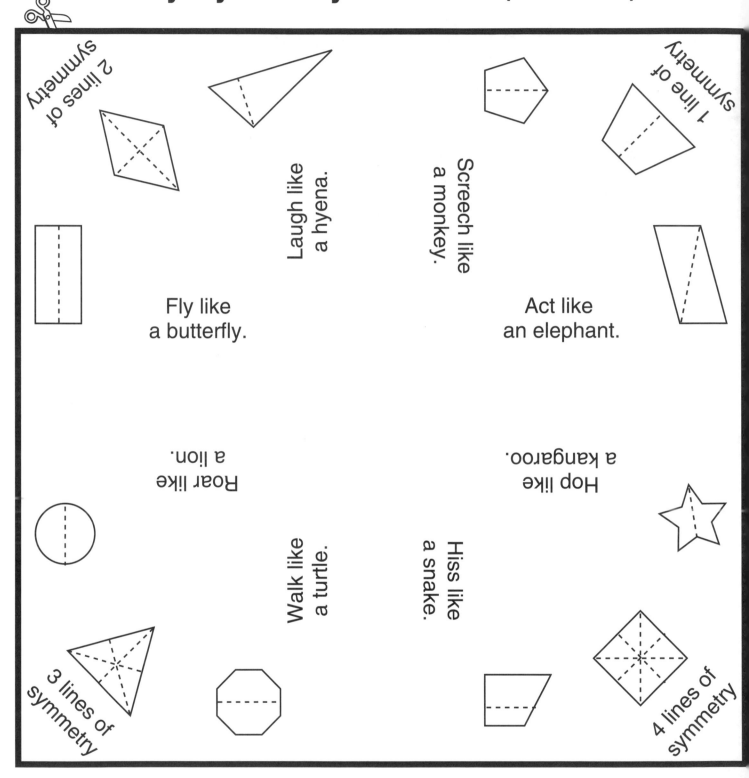

2 lines of symmetry

1 line of symmetry

Laugh like a hyena.

Screech like a monkey.

Fly like a butterfly.

Act like an elephant.

Roar like a lion.

Hop like a kangaroo.

Walk like a turtle.

Hiss like a snake.

3 lines of symmetry

4 lines of symmetry

TROUBLE AT THE TANGRAM ZOO

Objective

Students will use tangrams to create two-dimensional geometric shapes.

Anticipatory Set

Speak in an excited voice to students as if something very important has happened: "There's trouble at the Tangram Zoo! Last night, someone broke into the zoo, took the keys, and let all the animals out of their pens!" Throughout this lesson, treat students as if they are part of an exciting adventure to help increase motivation and interest.

Purpose

Tell students that their job is to help the zookeepers find all the animals. If they can solve the tangram puzzles and build all the animals, the zookeeper will be able to put the animals back in their pens. After all the animals are back in their pens, they will follow clues to solve a word puzzle and find out who took the keys and let out all the animals.

Input

Make copies of the tangram blocks on the top half of the **Animals at the Tangram Zoo reproducible (page 97).** Give each student a copy of the pattern blocks. While students are cutting apart the blocks, explain that a tangram is an ancient puzzle from China.

Modeling

Ask students if they have ever used tangrams before in school or in a game with friends. Ask them to describe their strategies of using the blocks to solve puzzles.

Trace the outline of the square on a transparency, and place it on the overhead. Invite students to watch as you place the tangram blocks on the transparency to form the square. Challenge students to use their own blocks to form the square at their desks.

Checking for Understanding

Walk around the room to see if everyone is able to make the square using their tangram blocks. Assist as needed.

Guided Practice

Divide the class into 12 groups. Have students take their tangram blocks with them. Then cut out the tangram animal cards on the bottom half of the Animals at the Tangram Zoo reproducible. (Do not give them the dinosaur picture at this time.) Give each group a picture of one animal. (You may wish to give every student in each group a copy of the same card for easier viewing.) Every group should have a different animal card.

Instruct students to work together in their groups and use their tangram blocks to form the animal. (Have students store their blocks in envelopes or resealable plastic bags to keep in their desks for later use.)

When students are finished, give them copies of the **Trouble at the Tangram Zoo reproducible (page 98).** Move from group to group, in order from 1 to 12, according to which animal each group formed with its blocks. Ask a volunteer from each group to name the animal and share a strategy used for building it.

Instruct students to complete the word puzzle using the names of all the animals in order from 1 to 12. They will then write the shaded letters in order from top to bottom on the lines below to solve the mystery about who took the keys and caused all the trouble at the zoo.

Closure

After the mystery is solved, place a transparency of the dinosaur puzzle on the overhead projector. Invite students to build it at their desks. Prompt them to write in their math journals about what they enjoyed most while working with tangram puzzles.

Independent Practice

For homework, give each student a copy of the Animals at the Tangram Zoo reproducible. Have each student take it home, cut out the tangram blocks, and build as many tangram animals as he or she can. Instruct students also to use the blocks to design their own projects. They can be animals, objects, or interesting designs. Have them trace the outlines of their designs and bring them to class. The next day, have each student share his or her design with a friend, and have students solve each other's tangram puzzles.

Animals at the Tangram Zoo

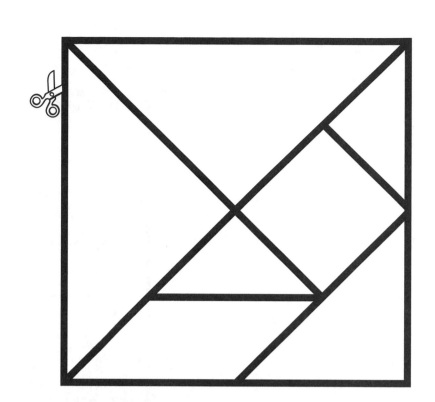

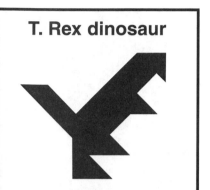

T. Rex dinosaur

1. cat	2. bear	3. eagle	4. fox
5. duck	**6. rabbit**	**7. flamingo**	**8. lion**
9. swan	**10. camel**	**11. skunk**	**12. giraffe**

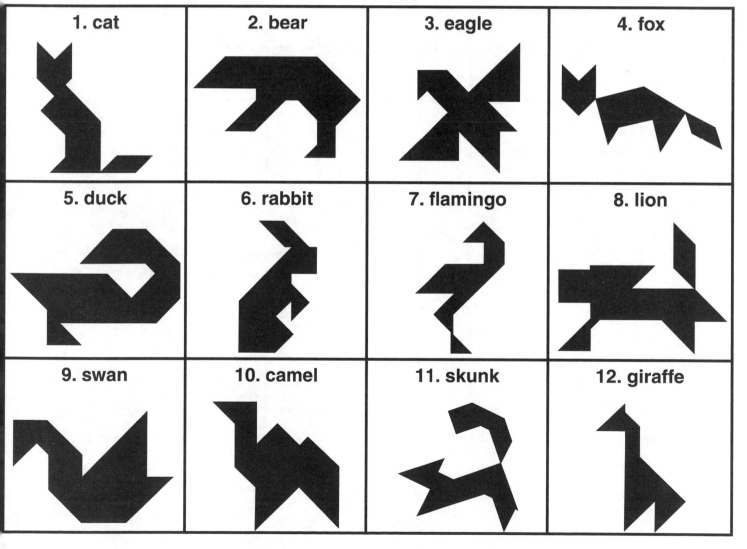

Trouble at the Tangram Zoo

Directions: Build each tangram animal. Then write the name of each animal in order from 1 to 12.

Directions: To solve the mystery, write the shaded letters from top to bottom on the lines below.

Who took the keys and let all the animals out of their pens?

___ ___ ___   ___ ___ ___ ___ ___   ___ ___ ___ ___ ___

MAGIC CARPETS FOR SALE

Objective

Students will construct models of paper rectangles to measure perimeter and area.

Anticipatory Set

Read aloud the text at the top of the **Magic Carpet Store reproducible (page 101).** For added fun, tell students that the genie promises to pay a bag of gold chocolate coins to the class if the students can make magic carpets the exact size he wants.

Purpose

Explain to students that they will work together in groups to make life-sized magic carpets for the genie using large sheets of butcher paper.

Input

Teach students how to find the perimeter and area of a rectangle. On the board, draw the rectangle from the first example on the **More Magic Carpets reproducible (page 102).** Label the sides, and say, "To find the perimeter of a rectangle, add the lengths of all four sides." Point out that the length of the rectangle is 6 ft (1.83 m) and the width is 4 ft (1.22 m). On the board, write "$P = l + w + l + w$." Under this equation, write "$P = 6 + 4 + 6 + 4$ ($P = 1.83$ m + 1.22 m + 1.83 m + 1.22 m)." Ask a volunteer to add the four numbers and write the answer: "$P = 20$ ft (6.1 m)."

Explain that there is a formula for finding the perimeter of a rectangle. Ask students to suggest a potential formula, and guide the discussion to conclude $P = 2l + 2w$. Find the perimeter using this formula.

Tell students, "To find the area of a rectangle, multiply the length and the width." On the board, write "$A = l \times w$." Under this equation, write "$A = 6 \times 4$ ($A = 1.83$ m $\times$ 1.22 m)." Ask a student to compute the equation and write the answer: "$A = 24$ ft^2 (2.23 m^2)."

Explain that you can also draw a picture on a piece of graph paper to find the area of a rectangle. Place a grid transparency on the overhead projector. Draw the rectangle used in this example on the grid. Count the number of squares inside the rectangle, and write "$A = 24$ ft^2 (2.23 m^2)."

Modeling

Provide students with graph paper. Instruct them to copy your work from the transparency. Draw the second example from the More Magic Carpets reproducible. Ask students to draw it on their graph paper and label the sides. Work together to find the perimeter and area of the rectangle. Use the formulas first, and then count the squares to check your answers.

Find the perimeter and area of several rectangles. Model how to use the formulas. Check answers by counting the squares.

Checking for Understanding

Walk around the room to check that everyone understands how to draw the rectangle on graph paper and find the perimeter and the area. Model more examples as needed.

Guided Practice

Give each student a copy of the Magic Carpet Store reproducible. Divide the class into small groups. Provide each group with a large sheet of butcher paper and a smaller sheet of butcher paper that measures 1 ft^2 (30.48 cm^2).

Assign each group a different length and width for its magic carpet. Be sure the carpet will fit on the butcher paper. Prompt students to follow the instructions on the reproducible to make the carpet with their groups. Tell them to write the perimeter and area of the carpet and record the measurements on the reproducible. If time allows, invite groups to decorate their magic carpets using crayons and markers.

Closure

After students have completed making and measuring their magic carpets, invite each group to show its carpet to the class. Tell students to write in their math journals about how they helped their groups make and measure their carpet. Then have them answer the following question: "What did I learn today in math class?" Reward the class for a job well done with the bag of chocolate coins that the genie promised.

Independent Practice

For homework, have students complete the More Magic Carpets reproducible. Remind them to use the correct formulas to find the answers.

Extending the Activity

Hang students' carpets around the classroom. Invite students to find the perimeter and area of each carpet.

Magic Carpet Store

Directions: You work in a store that makes magic
carpets. This morning, a genie came into the store. He
ordered a magic carpet just the right size for him to ride.
He told you the length and the width that he wanted.
Now it is your job to make it!

The genie wants his magic carpet to be

_____ feet/meters long and

_____ feet/meters wide.

1. Use your one-foot (30.48 cm) paper square to measure and draw the magic carpet
   on a large piece of paper.
2. Cut out the magic carpet.
3. Use the one-foot (30.48 cm) square to mark all the square feet on the carpet.
4. Measure the carpet, and record the measurements.

The perimeter of my magic carpet is _____.

The area of my magic carpet is _____.

5. Help decorate your magic carpet with crayons or markers.
6. Draw a picture of your magic carpet in the box below.

Name_____   Date_____

More Magic Carpets

Directions: The genie is back! He wants to buy more magic carpets. Find the perimeter and the area of each carpet the genie wants to buy.

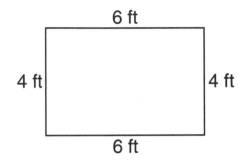

1. P = _____

   A = _____

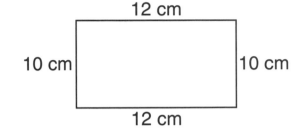

2. P = _____

   A = _____

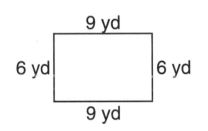

3. P = _____

   A = _____

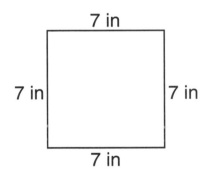

4. P = _____

   A = _____

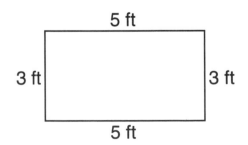

5. P = _____

   A = _____

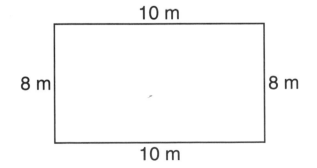

6. P = _____

   A = _____

GEO PUPPET

Objective

Students will analyze and compare the properties of plane figures and solid figures as they construct geometric puppets.

Anticipatory Set

Set up workstations with the following supplies: grid paper, pencils, rulers, compasses, scissors, white poster board, colored markers, hole punches, yarn and string, large metal washers, tape, and glue. Also supply wooden sticks (chopsticks, disposable stir sticks from paint stores, or craft sticks) for students to use to make handheld cross-sticks for their puppets.

Display an example of a completed geo puppet. Ask students, "What can you tell me about this puppet? How do you think math was used to make it?"

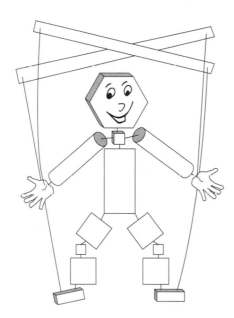

Purpose

Tell students that geometry is the study of shapes, including two-dimensional shapes, or *plane figures*, and three-dimensional shapes, or *solid figures*. In this activity, students will analyze and compare the attributes of plane and solid figures while they construct a string puppet made of geometric shapes.

Input

Review regular and irregular polygons with students, including the attributes of triangles (equilateral, isosceles, right), quadrilaterals (square, rectangle, rhombus, trapezoid), pentagons, hexagons, heptagons, octagons, nonagons, and decagons. Draw or show pictures of these figures, list the number of sides and angles for each one, and point out pairs of congruent or parallel sides (or angles).

Also review the attributes of solid figures, including pyramids (triangular sides with different polygon bases), prisms (rectangular sides with pairs of congruent polygon bases), cylinders, cones, and spheres. Explain that plane figures are flat, two-dimensional, closed figures with straight sides, whereas solid figures are three-dimensional and usually made of polygon faces (except for curved figures such as cylinders, cones, and spheres). Encourage students to ask questions and take notes in their math journals about these geometric concepts.

Modeling

Give each student a copy of the **Geo Puppet: Geometric Nets reproducible (page 106)** and several polygon and solid-figure blocks to examine and compare both visually and tactilely. Point out that each net is a flattened version of a solid figure that can be folded to construct that figure. Invite volunteers to name the polygons shown in each net and to match each net to the correct solid figure.

> Manipulatives can help students develop mental images of geometric shapes and visualize spatial relationships as well as improve their visual memory skills.

Refer to the sample puppet from the beginning of the lesson, and invite volunteers to identify the different solid figures used to make it. Explain that they will make their own geo puppets using nets of solid figures.

Guided Practice

Work together to write a list of solid figures used to make your sample puppet. Then demonstrate how to use grid paper and a ruler to draw large templates for two nets, such as the square pyramid and the cube. Point out that the nets on the reproducible are only for reference. The actual templates should be large enough to make a puppet at least 1 ft tall. Demonstrate how to count grid squares (perimeter and area) to draw congruent squares and triangles for each net.

After creating templates, demonstrate how to trace the templates onto poster board and cut out the shapes. Then punch a hole in the center of both the top and the bottom faces of the figures (for stringing). Fold and tape the edges together. Write the name of the solid figure on the bottom. Explain that each figure must be labeled with its geometric name.

Then demonstrate how to string the two solid figures together. Tie a washer at the bottom of each figure to secure it in place (so it does not slide down the string). If, after the figures are constructed, students realize they missed punching the appropriate holes, they can punch holes using ballpoint pens.

Finally, show students how to attach the figures (puppet's body parts) to the handheld cross-sticks, using different strings to connect the hands, feet, and head. Strings must be long enough for the puppet to hang and move naturally.

Checking for Understanding

Ask students to explain how to draw and use different templates to make a geo puppet. Ask questions such as, *How will you decide which solid figures to use for your puppet? How will you use the geometric nets to help you draw the templates?* and *How will you use grid-paper squares to make sure you are drawing congruent shapes for each net?*

Independent Practice

Have students work independently to plan and build their puppets. Direct them to begin by drawing rough sketches of their puppets and listing the needed geometric figures before creating templates. (They should include the following parts: head, neck, arms, hands, body/torso, legs, and feet.) Encourage students to refer to the Geo Puppet reproducible to create their solid figures. Be sure to check and approve sketches, lists, and templates before students begin construction.

Encourage students to experiment with different combinations of solid figures and lengths of string to make movable parts (e.g., a trio of congruent cubes for each leg). Suggest that they add details such as hair and clothing.

Closure

Invite students to share their geo puppets with the class. Ask them to explain how they made their puppets, naming the geometric figures used and showing how the puppet moves. Ask students to write step-by-step directions in their math journals for making their puppets, including the correct names of the geometric figures used.

Extending the Activity

Have students prepare and present puppet shows using their geo puppets for classmates or younger students. Invite them to work in small groups to write a script that includes appropriate math vocabulary.

Name_____   Date_____

Geo Puppet: Geometric Nets

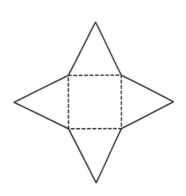

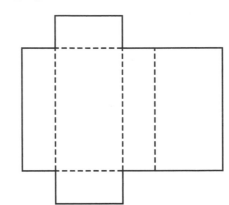

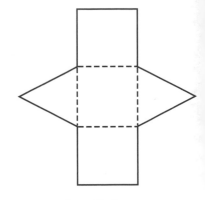

Square Pyramid:
1 square, 4 congruent triangles

Rectangular Prism: 3 pairs of congruent rectangles (top/bottom, front/back, side/side)

Triangular Prism:
3 congruent squares, 2 congruent triangles

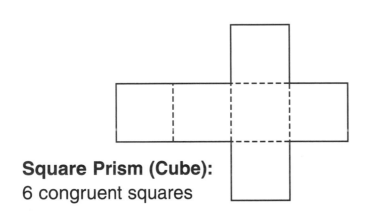

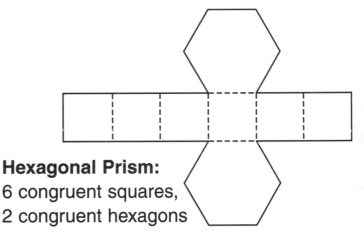

Square Prism (Cube):
6 congruent squares

Hexagonal Prism:
6 congruent squares, 2 congruent hexagons

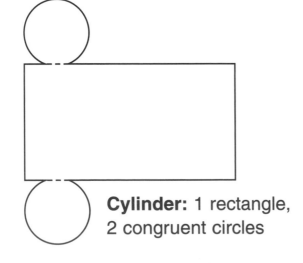

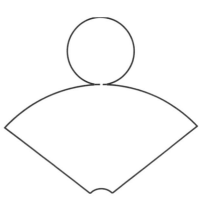

Cylinder: 1 rectangle, 2 congruent circles

Cone: 1 small circle, $\frac{1}{3}$ large circle

A HOLE IN THE ROOF

Objective

Students will measure and calculate the volume of various household containers.

Anticipatory Set

Display a variety of household containers, such as pots, pans, buckets, wastebaskets, bowls, cups, pitchers, flowerpots, and plastic storage boxes. Then tell students a short story: "The Emulov family has a 'little problem'—rainwater is pouring into their home through a hole in the roof. They are grabbing for these containers to catch the water and avoid a flood, but they do not know how much water each container will hold. How can they figure it out? For a hint, look for a clue in their name" (volume, *which is* Emulov *spelled backward*).

Purpose

Explain to students that *volume* is the amount of space inside a three-dimensional container. A container's volume is dependent on its length, width, and height. In this activity, students will help the Emulov family figure out how much water their containers will hold and how quickly those containers will fill.

Input

Display and compare solid figures, including cubes, prisms, pyramids, and cylinders. Remind students that there are different kinds of prisms and pyramids, such as rectangular prisms and triangular prisms, which are named according to the shape of their bases (flat bottoms or ends).

Ask students to write the following formulas for area and volume in their math journals. Explain that s stands for *side*, b stands for the bottom length of a triangle, h stands for *height*, B stands for the area of a polygon base (for a rectangular prism, $V = Bh = lwh$), r stands for *radius*, and π stands for *pi*, or 3.14.

Area (flat surface)	Volume (three-dimensional space)
Square $= s^2$	Cube $= s^3$
Rectangle $= lw$	Prism $= Bh$
Triangle $= \frac{1}{2} bh$	Pyramid $= \frac{1}{3} Bh$
Circle $= \pi r^2$	Cylinder $= \pi r^2 h$

Clarify that *area* is a measure of the space covered by a flat surface, such as a sheet of paper, whereas *volume* is a measure of how much something can hold inside of it, such as water inside a bottle.

Tell students that they will use the formulas for volume to calculate how much water each container on display can hold. They will also need these conversions (write them on the board for students to copy in their math journals):

- 1 cubic inch = 0.035 pint (1 cubic centimeter = 0.01 deciliter)
- 1 cubic inch = 0.0043 gallon (1 cubic centimeter = 0.001 liter)
- 2 cups = 1 pint (100 milliliters = 1 deciliter)
- 8 pints = 1 gallon (10 deciliters = 1 liter)

Modeling

> Have students use measurement tools to measure length, area, volume, mass, temperature, and other attributes of meaningful things in their environment. Ask students to estimate before they measure to build a stronger sense of measurement units and what they represent.

First, use a volume measurement set to help students understand the concept of volume. Show them how to fill the container with unit cubes to determine the volume. For example, if you have a three-in/cm cubed container, use 3×3 one-in/cm cubes to fill the bottom layer (area) of the container. Then stack two more layers of cubes to show that $3 \times (3 \times 3) = 27$ in^3/cm^3 is the volume of the container.

Next, demonstrate how to measure and calculate the volume of one container on display, using a customary ruler to measure dimensions to the nearest ½ in/cm (point out approximate measurements for containers with rounded corners or narrowing widths). Plug those values into the appropriate formula to calculate the volume of the container. For example, for an 8 in/cm $\times$ 4.5 in/cm $\times$ 4 in/cm rectangular container, $V = Bh = lwh = 8$ in/cm $\times$ 4.5 in/cm $\times$ 4 in/cm $= 144$ in^3/cm^3.

Show students how to convert volume to pints or gallons of water (or deciliters or liters). For example, since 1 in^3 = 0.035 pt (1 cm^3 = 0.01 dL), then 144 in^3 = 144 $\times$ 0.035 = 5.04 pt (144 cm^3 = 144 $\times$ 0.01 = 1.44 dL), which is about 5 pt or a little more than ½ gal (1 ½ dL or about 1/10 L).

Guided Practice

Divide the containers into equal groups so teams of students can measure them and calculate each volume. Have teams use calculators and measuring tape or rulers and meter sticks to determine how much water each container can hold. Remind students to refer to the example on the board and to use the appropriate volume formulas.

Guide students' progress, circulating around the room and assisting as needed. Have teams record their results on the board, writing the formula and the measurements used to calculate the volume of each container. Then have teams trade containers and check each other's work. If a team disagrees with a previous result, have that team use a different-colored marker to show its results next to those on the board.

Checking for Understanding

Review and discuss the results together, encouraging students to find and correct any mistakes. Ask a volunteer to summarize how to calculate the amount of water each container can hold (*Measure the dimensions in inches, use the appropriate formula to calculate the volume in cubic inches, and then convert to pints or gallons.*). Ask, "How much water can the Emulov family catch with all of the containers combined?" (*Add the gallons.*).

Independent Practice

For homework, have students write a comical, illustrated math story about the Emulov family's using a variety of household containers to catch rainwater leaking through their roof. They must include volume, measurement, and other math calculations in their stories.

Closure

Ask students to share and read aloud their math stories. Encourage them to stop and ask their audience for solutions to the math problems before they give the answers. Display students' stories on a bulletin board, or bind them to make a class book. Invite students to share in their math journals their thoughts about the activity and how it helped them learn new math concepts.

Extending the Activity

Have students use metric units instead of customary units (or customary units instead of metric units) to calculate the volume of different containers. Have them record and use these conversions: $1 \text{ cm}^3 = 1 \text{ mL}$; $1,000 \text{ mL} = 1 \text{ L}$; $1 \text{ L} = 0.26 \text{ gal}$; $3.8 \text{ L} = 231 \text{ in}^3$.

FROM FARM TO FACTORY

Objective

Students will use measurement skills to investigate the process of apple farming.

Anticipatory Set

Show students pictures of apple farms and baskets of apples. Explain that more than 50 million tons (45 million megagrams or tonnes) of apples are grown worldwide each year. Invite students to name some of their favorite apple products, such as apple pies, apple tarts, applesauce, and dried apples. Then ask, "How do you think math is used to produce apples? How do you think those apples get from farms to factories and stores?"

Purpose

Tell students that apple farmers use a variety of math skills, such as measuring and packaging different numbers of apples to sell at stores. In this activity, students will learn more about how math is used to produce and sell apples.

Input

Display and discuss the following apple farm facts with students. Review the meaning of the inequality symbol ($\geq$), and review how to convert one unit of measure to another. For example, 1 ha of land $= 2\frac{1}{2}$ acres $= 2\frac{1}{2}$ $(43,560 \text{ ft}^2) = 108,900 \text{ ft}^2$ (1 ha of land $= 0.01 \text{ km}^2 = 0.01 \text{ km}^2 \times 1,000,000 \text{ m}^2 = 10,000 \text{ m}^2$) of land. Point out that the first fact states the area of land (length $\times$ width) needed for each apple tree, which is 20 ft $\times$ 20 ft $= 400 \text{ ft}^2$ (6.1 m $\times$ 6.1 m $= 37.21 \text{ m}^2$).

Apple Farm Facts

- Apple trees are planted 20 $\times$ 20 ft (6.1 $\times$ 6.1 m) apart.
- 1 acre of land $= 43,560 \text{ ft}^2$ (4046.86 m^2).
- 1 ha of land $= 2\frac{1}{2}$ acres ($10,000 \text{ m}^2$).
- Each tree yields 100 to 200 apples.
- Apples with a diameter $\geq 2\frac{1}{2}$ in (6.35 cm) are sellable.

Remind students that volume is the amount of space or capacity inside a three-dimensional figure (measured in cubic units). Review the following formulas for volume. Tell students that they will need to know how to calculate different volumes for this activity.

- Rectangular prism $= lwh$
- Cylinder $= \pi r^2 h$
- Sphere $= \frac{4}{3} \pi r^3$

Modeling

Place a brown paper lunch bag (rectangular prism) next to an apple. Ask students, "Suppose you are using this bag to collect apples in your apple orchard. About how many apples do you think will fit inside the bag? How can you use this apple to estimate the number? How can you use this apple and bag to estimate the total number of bags needed for all the apples in your orchard?" To estimate the total number of bags, you must calculate the approximate volume of the apple, the volume of the bag, and the approximate number of apples in the entire orchard.

Ask students, "What is the best formula for calculating the volume of an apple, the space it will fill inside the bag?" (*sphere*). "What is the best formula for calculating the volume of the bag, the space inside?" (*rectangular prism*). Point out that apples aren't exactly spherical, but you can use the formula for a sphere to get an approximate volume. Demonstrate how to use a ruler or measuring tape to measure the dimensions of the apple (radius or diameter) and the dimensions of the bag (length, width, height). Then calculate the volumes using the formulas for a sphere ($V = \frac{4}{3}\pi r^3$) and rectangular prism ($V = lwh$).

Fill the bag with apples to compare the actual number to the estimate. Ask students, "Why might the actual number be slightly different than the estimate?" Remind students that apples aren't exactly spherical. They also vary in size, which is why the actual number might be slightly more or less.

Then ask, "Suppose there are 2,000 apples in your orchard. How can you calculate about how many total bags you will need to collect all the apples?" Show students how to divide 2,000 by the number of apples per bag to get the answer.

> By simply adding a visual representation of a situation that is relevant to students, greater meaning can be obtained.

Guided Practice

Give each student a copy of the **From Farm to Factory reproducible (pages 113–114)** and a calculator. Read aloud the directions, farm facts, and collection containers data. Then show students how to use the facts and formulas to calculate and solve the first three problems:

- "Which facts do we need to solve the first problem?" (*first three facts*). "If we convert the number of hectares to square feet, how can we determine how many trees fit on the orchard?" (*Divide: 108,900 ft² of land ÷ 400 ft² per tree = 272 trees or 10,000 m² of land ÷ 37.21 m² per tree = 268.74 trees*).
- "Why can't we calculate the exact number of apples per tree for the second problem?" (*The number of apples produced always varies from year to year.*). "How do you think the value of 100 to 200 apples was determined?" (*Possible answer: By comparing the average number of apples produced from year to year.*).
- "How is the third problem similar to the example we did together? Where do we get the dimensions for each container listed?" (*Look at the*

Collection Containers information.). "What two formulas do we need to determine how many apples fit inside the bag? The basket? The other containers?" (*For the apple, use the formula for the volume of a sphere. For the containers, use the formula for either a rectangular prism or a cylinder, depending on the shape.*).

Checking for Understanding

Tell students that some of the remaining problems on the page may require answers from previous problems solved. Read aloud problems 4, 5, and 6. Ask, "Besides the factual information and the formulas in your math journals, what other information do you need to solve these problems? Do you use the minimum number of apples from problem 2 or the maximum number? Why?" (*Use the maximum number of apples to estimate the greatest number of containers, weight, or truckloads needed.*).

Independent Practice

For homework, have students complete the From Farm to Factory reproducible. Remind them to use the formulas in their math journals and refer to the problems done in class. For the last problem, ask students to think about other situations a farmer might face, such as the effects of weather conditions or pest control. The next day, have partners check and compare answers before going over the answers together as a class. Invite volunteers to read aloud the problems on the back of their papers and ask classmates to try to solve them.

Closure

Invite students to answer these questions in their math journals: "What did you learn from this activity? Do you think it was a good way to help you learn math? Why or why not?"

From Farm to Factory

Directions: Congratulations! You are the proud owner of an apple farm that is ready for harvest. Solve each problem to find out how much money you will make from your apple crop.

Apple Farm Facts

- Apple trees are planted 20 ft × 20 ft apart.
- 1 acre of land = 43,560 square feet.
- 1 hectare (ha) of land = $2\frac{1}{2}$ acres.
- Each tree yields 100 to 200 apples.
- Apples with a diameter ≥ $2\frac{1}{2}$" are sellable.

Collection Containers

- Rectangular bag: $l = 6$", $w = 4$", $h = 16$".
- Cylindrical "bushel" basket: $d = 18\frac{1}{2}$", $h = 8$".
- Rectangular carton: $l = 15$", $w = 12$", $h = 10$".
- Cylindrical barrel: $d = 24$", $h = 36$".
- Rectangular bin: $l = 36$", $w = 40$", $h = 24$".

1. Your apple orchard is 1 hectare in size. About how many trees are in the orchard?

_____

2. If each tree produces 100 to 200 apples, what is the minimum number of apples

you can expect from your orchard? _____ What is the

maximum number? _____

From Farm to Factory (Continued)

3. If each apple is at least $2\frac{1}{2}$ inches in diameter, about how many apples will fit in each kind of container?
   Hint: First estimate the volume per apple using the formula for a sphere.

   Bag: _____ Barrel: _____

   Basket: _____ Bin: _____

   Carton: _____

4. If you use only cartons to package your apples for delivery to stores and factories, about how many cartons will you need for your entire apple crop? _____

5. If each apple weighs about $\frac{1}{4}$ pound (lb.), about how many pounds will your entire apple crop weigh? _____

6. If a truck can hold about 2 tons (1 ton = 2,000 lbs.) of apples, about how many truckloads will you need to deliver all your apples to stores and factories? _____

7. If you get paid 50% of the retail price for apples (the price sold in stores), and the retail price is $3.00/lb., about how much money could you earn for your entire crop? _____

8. If half the amount of money you earn must be used to pay for all your expenses (materials, equipment, hired help, shipping, delivery), how much money will you have left (what is your profit)? _____

9. What might affect the actual amount you get for your crop? Consider both the yield of apples (the number of apples collected) and the money paid.

   _____

   _____

10. On the back of this paper, write your own multistep math problem about apple farming that involves measurement. Then show how to solve your problem.

WRAPPING UP MATH

Objective

Students will measure and find the surface area of different sizes of gift boxes.

Anticipatory Set

Collect cardboard gift boxes of various sizes and shapes, grouping together identical sets for each group of students. Write a different letter on the boxes in each set. Use the same letters for identical boxes across sets (e.g., write "A" on the 9 × 12 in [22.86 × 30.48 cm] gift box in each set).

Display a set of boxes, and present the following situation to students: "Suppose you are working at a department store as a gift wrapper. You have been asked to purchase just enough wrapping paper to wrap these boxes without having any paper leftover. How could you determine the exact amount of paper to purchase to cover these boxes?"

Purpose

Tell students that they can determine exactly how much paper they need to cover each box by calculating the *surface area*, the total area of all the flat surfaces (*faces*) of the box. In this activity, students will work in teams to measure and calculate the surface area of each gift box in a set to determine how much gift wrap they need.

Input

Review the following formulas for the area of regular polygons. Remind students that the opposite sides of rectangles and squares are parallel and congruent.

- Rectangle = lw
- Square = s^2

- Triangle = $\frac{1}{2} bh$
- Trapezoid = $\frac{1}{2} h(base\ a + base\ b)$

Tell students that sometimes they must find the area of irregular shapes, which are usually a combination of regular polygons. Draw a block letter T with the following labeled lengths: 12 in/cm, 3 in/cm, 4 in/cm, 6 in/cm, 4 in/cm, 6 in/cm, 4 in/cm, 3 in/cm. Show students how to draw a line to divide the letter into two rectangles, top and bottom. Demonstrate how to find the lengths of unlabeled parts by referring to the congruency of opposite sides of a rectangle. For example, since the top of the T is 12 in/cm, the missing measurement of the opposite side must be 4 in/cm to get a total of 12 in/cm (4 in/cm + 4 in/cm + 4 in/cm = 12 in/cm).

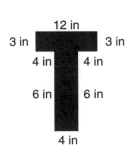

Show how to calculate the area of the top rectangle ($l \times w$ = 12 in/cm × 3 in/cm = 36 in²/cm²) and the bottom rectangle ($l \times w$ = 6 in/cm × 4 in/cm = 24 in²/cm²). Add the products to get the total area: 36 in²/cm² + 24 in²/cm² = 60 in²/cm².

Explain that you could also calculate the total area of the *T*, dividing it into three vertical rectangles, a long middle rectangle flanked by two congruent rectangles. Both methods yield the same surface area.

Modeling

Show students one of the rectangular gift boxes disassembled and flattened. Label each part (face) with a different number, such as A1, A2, A3, A4, A5, and A6 for gift box A. By finding the area of each part and then adding those products, you can determine the total surface area of the box. This is the amount of gift wrap needed.

Model how to use a ruler to measure the sides of each part. List each measurement on the board. Point out that the opposite faces of a rectangular prism are congruent, so you need to find the area of only one face for each pair and then double that number.

Checking for Understanding

Ask students, "If you had a cube-shaped box, what would be the quickest way to find the surface area?" Guide them to realize that they need to measure and calculate the area for only one face and multiply by six since all six faces of a cube are congruent.

Guided Practice

Give each team of students a set of gift boxes, rulers, scissors, and calculators. Monitor students' progress as they disassemble each box, measure each part, and use those measurements to find the total surface area. Tell them to record their work in their math journals. Encourage teammates to check each other's work.

Closure

Have teams share their results and confirm the correct answers. Encourage students to identify and explain any incorrect results (e.g., inaccurate measuring, wrong formulas, incorrect calculations).

Independent Practice

For homework, have students write and solve their own math problems by drawing block letters for *E, F, H, I, L,* and *T*. Tell them to measure and label the length of each side (metric or customary units) and then calculate the surface area of each letter. The next day, have students exchange papers and check each other's work.

4

Algebra

SIMPLY, SIMPLIFY

Objective

Students will learn how to simplify mathematic expressions.

Anticipatory Set

Write five expressions separately on the board, such as 846, 3 + 5, 25 + (20 + 5), (15 − 5) + 48, and 14 + (23 − 22) + (60 − 55). Ask volunteers to describe what they see on the board. Guide the discussion to include such terms as *numbers, addition signs, subtraction signs,* and *parentheses.*

Purpose

Tell students, "These numbers and addition and subtraction signs may seem confusing because there are so many." Explain that students will learn how to make these examples as simple as possible.

Ask students to share about a time when something seemed very confusing or complicated and someone helped to simplify it for them. Suggest situations such as following instructions for building a model, cooking a recipe, or following directions on a map. Invite students to share how they felt after the situation was simplified.

Input

Tell students that each of these examples is known as an *expression.* In mathematics, an expression can be one number. An expression can include numbers as well as addition, subtraction, multiplication, and division signs. An expression can also have parentheses.

Explain, "When you see an expression, it is important to try to simplify it. There are rules to follow when simplifying an expression. First, simplify the work inside the parentheses. Then, finish the rest of the problem starting at the left and moving to the right."

Modeling

Using the first two examples on the **Just Simplify! reproducible (page 120)** as a guide, simplify each of the five expressions on the board. Show students how to do the work inside the parentheses first. Draw arrows to demonstrate how each number is used in the next step of the problem. Your work should resemble a triangle with the answer written at the bottom.

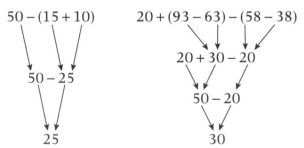

Checking for Understanding

Ask volunteers to provide a definition of *expression,* and then explain the two rules to follow when simplifying an expression. Check to make sure everyone understands the concept. Model more examples as needed.

Guided Practice

Divide the class into groups of five or six students. Invite each student to write an expression on a piece of paper. Have students pass their papers to the left and simplify each other's expressions. Tell them to write each step and show their work.

Instruct each student to write another expression and then pass his or her paper to a different student in the group. Have students simplify each other's expressions. Repeat the activity several times, with students exchanging papers with new group members each time.

Closure

Ask students how following the rules helped them to simplify the expressions. Prompt students to write in their math journals about what they learned and how simplifying math expressions might help to alleviate the pressure of facing complicated math problems. Ask students, "What other things do you do that are easier when you break them down into steps?"

In closure, the student does most of the work by mentally rehearsing and summarizing those concepts and deciding whether they made sense and have meaning.

Independent Practice

Distribute copies of the Just Simplify! reproducible for homework. Read the comic strip together first, and discuss any questions before students take it home.

Just Simplify!

Directions: Simplify each expression. Work inside the parentheses first. Then work from left to right.

1. $50 - (15 + 10)$

   $50 - \underline{}$

   $\underline{}$

2. $20 + (93 - 63) - (58 - 38)$

   $20 + \underline{} - \underline{}$

   $\underline{} - \underline{}$

   $\underline{}$

Directions: Simplify each expression on a separate sheet of paper.

3. $(17 + 3) + (65 - 55) + 10$

4. $(87 - 57) + 30$

5. $30 + (68 - 8) - 70$

6. $(58 + 2) + (74 - 64) - 30$

7. $(47 - 1) - (20 + 23) + 15$

8. $(104 - 4) - (16 + 4) + 2$

9. $8 + (52 - 22)$

10. $76 - (6 + 50) - 8$

WEIGH TO GO!

Objective

Students will learn to write an equation using two expressions.

Anticipatory Set

Display a balance scale for students. (If you do not have a balance scale in the classroom, make a simple one by hanging two matching paper cups from string on opposite ends of a hanger.) Place two objects of equal weight on the scale. Invite students to share their observations. Guide the discussion to conclude that these items are *equal*. Remove those items, and place two objects of different weights on the scale. Invite students to share their observations. Guide the discussion to conclude that these items are *not equal*.

Purpose

Tell students that they will be comparing different mathematical expressions. They will be simplifying the expressions to see if they have equal value. Explain, "Just as some objects on a scale are *equal*, some expressions are *equal*. And just as some objects on a scale are *not equal*, some expressions are *not equal*."

Input

Using the **Equal—or *Not!* reproducible (page 123)** as a guide, write the two expressions from the first problem on the board: "$(15 + 15) - 5$" and "$10 + (7 + 8)$." Simplify. Explain that since both expressions have the same value, you can write an equation using an equal sign. Write the equation: "$(15 + 15) - 5 = 10 + (7 + 8)$."

Next, write the two expressions, "$20 - (10 - 8)$" and "$(10 - 5) + 10$." Simplify. Explain that since the expressions do not have the same value, you can write the equal sign in a way that shows the expressions are not equal. Write the equation: "$20 - (10 - 8) \neq (10 - 5) + 10$." Point out that the first expression is not equal to the second expression. They do not have the same value.

> Teach the new material first after getting the students' focus. This is the time of greatest retention.

Modeling

On the board, write the two expressions from the second problem on the Equal—or *Not!* reproducible. Simplify both expressions. Ask students if both expressions have the same value (*yes*). Ask a volunteer which symbol should be used to write the expressions in an equation (=). Write the equation on the board: "$3 + (6 + 1) = (12 - 6) + 4$."

Next, ask students to draw an equal sign (=) and a not equal sign ($\neq$) on separate sheets of paper. Write an equation on the board that has two expressions. Use those from the reproducible, or create your own. Then simplify the expressions. Ask students to show which symbol should be used in the equation by holding up the correct sign. Tell them to keep their eyes straight ahead so they cannot peek at their classmates' answers. Repeat this process several times until students have a good understanding of the concept.

Checking for Understanding

Ensure that students understand how to use the two signs for equal and not equal. Model more equations on the board if needed.

Guided Practice

Tell students they will play a game similar to Four Corners. Prepare index cards by writing different equations on them. Use equations from the reproducible, or create your own. Write only equal signs in the equations. Place all the cards in a box or bag. Then post four of the students' equal/not equal papers in four corners of the room.

Instruct students to stand in a corner of their choice next to one of the signs. Draw one card from the bag. Write the equation on the board. Simplify the expression. Ask a volunteer to identify which symbol should be used in the equation. Write the symbol on the board. All students standing in the corner with the matching symbol stay in the game. All others must return to their seats.

For the next round, direct students to stand in a different corner. Invite volunteers who are seated to draw a card from the bag, write the equation on the board, and simplify the expressions. All students standing in the corner with the matching symbol stay in the game. All others must return to their seats. Continue playing the game until there is one student left—the winner.

Closure

Review the lesson. Have students describe the steps for simplifying expressions in their math journals. Invite them to draw pictures of both symbols, = and ≠.

Independent Practice

Reinforce the concept of simplifying expressions in equations by having students complete the Equal—or *Not!* reproducible for homework.

Equal—or *Not!*

Directions: Simplify each expression. If the expressions in the equation have the same value, leave the equal symbol as is. If the expressions do not have the same value, change the symbol to show that the first expression is *not equal to* the second.

EQUAL

=

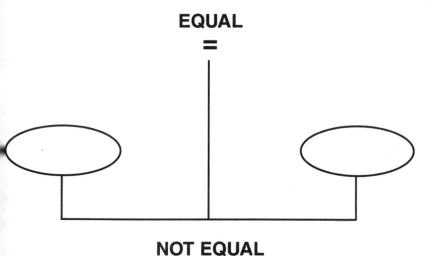

NOT EQUAL

≠

1. $(15 + 15) - 5 = 10 + (7 + 8)$

2. $3 + (6 + 1) = (12 - 6) + 4$

3. $20 - (10 - 8) = (10 - 5) + 10$

4. $(30 - 10) + 1 = 10 + (8 + 2)$

5. $(2 + 3) + 1 = 4 + (10 - 2)$

6. $8 + (10 - 3) = 10 + (18 - 13)$

7. $15 - (6 - 2) = (8 + 2) + 1$

8. $(7 + 2) + 10 = 5 + (13 - 3)$

9. $12 + (23 - 20) = 7 + (15 - 7)$

Directions: Simplify the expressions in the space below. Write the correct symbol to show if the expressions are *equal* or *not equal.*

10. $(59 + 1) + (28 - 8) + 3 = (72 + 8) - (14 - 4) + 9$

WHAT'S THE SCORE?

Objective

Students will learn to identify an inequality by simplifying two expressions.

Anticipatory Set

Past experience always affects new learning.

Invite students to share about sports teams on which they play or favorite football, basketball, or baseball teams they follow and like to watch. Ask them to tell about a time the score was close but then one team pulled ahead to win. Ask students, "How important is it to know which score is *greater than* or *less than* the other score?"

Purpose

Invite students to imagine they are at a baseball game and the scorekeeper is held up in traffic. Tell them it is their job to add up the scores. They need to find out which team's score is greater than or less than the other score so they can find out who won the game.

Input

Write the names of two baseball teams on the board. Name two teams students play on, or list professional sports teams such as the Pirates and Dodgers. Write an expression under "Pirates": "(2 + 3) + 1." Say, "In the second inning, the Pirates scored two runs and then scored three more. Then in the ninth inning, they scored one more run."

Under "Dodgers," write an expression of a different value: "4 + (1 + 4)." Say, "In the fourth inning, the Dodgers scored four runs. In the eighth inning, they scored one run and then four more." Invite students to help you simplify the expressions. Then say, "When two expressions have different values, you can write an *inequality.*" Draw the less than (<) and greater than (>) symbols on the board. Explain their meanings.

Write the inequality "(2 + 3) + 1 < 4 + (1 + 4)" on the board. Explain that the smaller end of the symbol always points to the smaller value and the open end always points to the larger value. Distinguishing the less than symbol from the greater than symbol can be confusing for some students. Show them how to use their left hands to form the less than symbol and their right hands to form the greater than symbol. Say, "The Pirates's score is less than the Dodgers's score. Six is less than nine. (2 + 3) + 1 is less than 4 + (1 + 4)."

Modeling

Tell students that the two teams played again the next day, but this time, the scorekeeper was sick. Tell students it is their job to add up the expressions and determine whose score was greater. Repeat the previous activity, and model the example with two new expressions. For the Pirates, write "2 + (3 + 3)" on the board. For the Dodgers, write "$3 + (1 + 1)$." Simplify the two expressions. Then write the inequality on the board: "$2 + (3 + 3) > 3 + (1 + 1)$." Invite students to show the greater than symbol using their right hands.

Checking for Understanding

Write another example of an inequality on the board using two expressions. Ask students to show the greater than or less than symbol using their hands to check for understanding. Model more examples as needed.

Guided Practice

Invite students to choose partners to play a card game. Give each student a set of the cards cut out from the **What's the Score? Game Cards reproducible (page 126)**. (You may wish to glue the cards to index cards or laminate them for durability.)

How to Play the Game

To play the game, players sit side by side. Each player has a deck of cards, a pencil, and scratch paper. Each player shuffles his or her own deck, places it facedown in a pile, and places the two symbol cards faceup to the side.

Each player turns over one card from his or her own deck and places it next to the other player's as if they were making an equation or an inequality. Players then work together to simplify the expressions and determine which expression is greater than the other. They place the correct symbol between the expressions to form either an equation or an inequality.

The player with the expression of greater value collects both cards and adds them to the bottom of his or her pile. If the expressions have the same value, the cards stay on the table. Players take another turn until they get an inequality. The player with the larger expression collects all the cards and adds them to the bottom of his or her pile. The player who collects the most cards wins the game.

Closure

After playing the game, have students write brief stories in their math journals about a sports game in which each team scored a different number of points across innings or quarters. Have them write inequalities using two expressions to show the final score.

Independent Practice

For homework, have students take home their decks of cards. Tell them to write 10 examples of inequalities using the expressions on the cards.

What's the Score? Game Cards

>	=	3 + (18 – 8)
(20 – 8) – 4		(12 + 3) – 6
(10 + 10) – 5		19 – (23 – 20)
(26 – 22) + 3		8 + (16 – 14)
(8 + 7) + 5		(8 + 4) + 2
4 + (9 – 2)		20 – (7 + 1)

SUNKEN TREASURE

Objective

Students will learn to complete a function table to help them determine the answer for an unknown variable.

Anticipatory Set

Gain students' attention by explaining that today's lesson will be about people finding sunken treasure on a deep-sea diving exhibition. Say, "One day, two friends named Chelsea and Mario went deep-sea diving. Deep, deep down in the ocean, they found a treasure chest filled with gold! Chelsea grabbed 12 gold coins. Mario grabbed 5 fewer coins than Chelsea. Then they both swam back to their boat."

Purpose

Have students imagine they are newspaper reporters interviewing Chelsea and Mario about their exciting adventure. They already know that Mario grabbed five fewer gold coins than did Chelsea. Their goal is to find out how many coins Mario grabbed and report it in the news.

Input

Write the equation "$c - 5 = m$" on the board. Explain that c stands for the number of gold coins Chelsea grabbed. The letter m stands for the number of gold coins Mario grabbed. Tell students, "We know how many coins Chelsea grabbed. Let's write that number for the value of c." Write "$12 - 5 = m$." Explain that you can now solve the equation to find the value of m. Write "$m = 7$" on the board. Invite a volunteer to share what he or she would report in the news about Chelsea and Mario's deep-sea diving adventure.

Using the function tables on the **Sunken Treasure reproducible (page 129)** as a guide, draw a function table on the board. Instruct students to copy all board work onto a sheet of paper. Label the left column "c," and label the right column "m." Over the table, write "$c - 5 = m$." Explain that a *function table* can be used to help find the value of one variable in an equation when you already know the value of another variable.

Modeling

Model how to use a function table. Write "12" in the first row under the c column. Ask students, "If Chelsea grabbed 12 coins, how many coins did Mario grab?" (*7*). Write "13," "14," "15," and "16" in the remaining four rows in the c column. Then ask, "If Chelsea grabbed 13 coins, how many coins did Mario grab? We can use the equation to find the new value of m by substituting the new value of c." Explain that if Chelsea grabbed 13 coins, then Mario grabbed 8. Write the answer in the m column.

Continue to model how to complete the function table. Use examples from the Sunken Treasure reproducible to model several more function tables on the board, instructing students to copy your work.

Checking for Understanding

Walk around the room, and check students' work to see that they are completing the function tables correctly. Invite volunteers to explain strategies they used to complete the tables.

Guided Practice

Tell each student to imagine he or she went deep-sea diving with a friend and found a treasure chest filled with gold coins, just like Chelsea and Mario did. Draw a blank function table on the board. Instruct students to copy the table onto new sheets of paper. Have each student label one column of the table with his or her initial and the other column with the friend's initial.

Invite each student to choose how many more or fewer coins he or she grabbed than the friend. Tell students to choose a number between 1 and 20. If a student grabbed *more* coins than his or her friend, the expression would be similar to $c = m + 3$, where the m stands for the friend's name. If he or she grabbed *fewer* coins than the friend, the expression would be similar to $c = m - 3$. Note that expressions will differ depending on the number of coins grabbed. Instruct each student to write the equation above his or her function table. Then have each student write four values for the column under his or her initial and leave the other column blank.

Direct students to switch function tables with partners. Allow time for them to complete their partners' tables to find the values for the variables.

Closure

Tell students to copy their completed function tables into their math journals. Then ask them to write short stories about their deep-sea diving adventures. Allow time for them to share their stories with the class.

Independent Practice

For homework, have students complete a copy of the Sunken Treasure reproducible and answer the questions at the bottom of the page.

Name_____   Date_____

Sunken Treasure

One day, four friends went deep-sea diving. They found a sunken treasure chest filled with gold! Each friend grabbed a handful of gold coins and swam back to the boat. When they counted their coins, Anna had four fewer coins than Ben. Dan had three more coins than Courtney. Courtney had two more coins than Ben.

Directions: Look at the function tables. Each letter represents the first letter of each friend's name. Complete each function table. Use the information to answer the questions below.

1. a = b − 4

a	b
4	
5	
6	
7	

2. a + 6 = c

a	c
	8
	10
	12
	14

3. a = d − 9

a	d
11	
9	
7	
5	

4. b + 2 = c

b	c
	10
	13
	14
	19

5. b = d − 5

b	d
	25
	20
	15
	10

6. c + 3 = d

c	d
7	
8	
9	
10	

7. If Anna got 6 gold coins, how many coins did Ben get? _____

8. If Anna got 9 gold coins, how many coins did Dan get? _____

9. If Dan got 25 gold coins, how many coins did Ben get? _____

10. If Courtney got 10 gold coins, how many coins did Dan get?_____

5

Data Analysis

Terrific T's

Our Favorite Things

Book Bonanza

Too Many Ants!

Survey Study

Fast Food Comparisons

Parachute Drop

Plot the Treasure

Animal Olympics

TERRIFIC T'S

Objective

Students will display data on glyphs and learn to identify the mode.

Anticipatory Set

Draw a large number line on the board from 0 to 10, spacing out the numbers as far as possible. Ask students, "How many pets to you have at your house?" Invite several volunteers to find the number on the board and stand in front of it. On the overhead projector, draw a line plot that shows the results. Have students return to their seats.

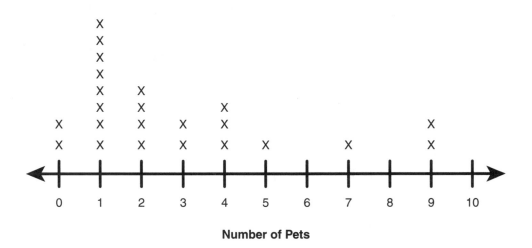

Number of Pets

Purpose

Tell students that they will learn more about each other by collecting data. They will be answering questions about themselves and then organizing the data on plots and graphs.

Input

Draw students' attention to the line plot on the overhead. Explain that the *mode* is a number that occurs the most in a set of data. Invite students to look at the line plot. Point out the number on the line plot that has more Xs than the others and say, "This number is the *mode.*"

Modeling

Ask students, "How many aunts do you have?" Invite several volunteers to find the number on the number line and stand in front of it. On the overhead, draw a new line plot that shows the results. Have students return to their seats.

Ask students to look at the line plot for this new data set: "Which number on the line plot has more Xs above it than the others?" Remind them that this number is the mode. Repeat this activity several times, asking a different question each time. For each new line plot, invite a volunteer to identify the mode.

Checking for Understanding

Ask students to explain the definition of *mode*. Draw a new line plot on the overhead. Name each number, and ask students to raise their hands if they think that number is the mode. Continue to model more line plots as needed.

Guided Practice

Give each student a copy of the **Terrific T's Glyph reproducible (page 134)**. Then place a transparency of the **Terrific T's Legend reproducible (page 135)** on the overhead. Explain that students will be decorating their T-shirts to display data. Read the directions for the buttons together. Allow time for students to draw buttons on their T-shirts accordingly. Then read the directions for the stripes together. Allow time for students to draw stripes. Continue reading through the directions together as students complete their glyphs.

When finished, ask students, "How many brothers and sisters do you have?" Direct them to take their glyphs with them to find the number on the number line and stand in front of it. Instruct students within each line to check each other's work to see that they have the correct number of buttons drawn on their glyphs.

Draw a line plot on the overhead to represent the results. Have students return to their seats. Then refer to the line plot to find the mode.

Repeat this process with the number of sisters, number of brothers, and number of letters in their first names. Each time students stand at the number line, have them check each other's work. After they return to their seats, identify the mode for that line plot on the overhead.

Closure

Invite students to share their glyphs with the class. Then ask them to write in their math journals about what they learned about line plots and glyphs. Display students' glyphs on a colorful bulletin board, and discuss the results.

Independent Practice

For homework, instruct students to take a simple survey and collect data. Have them ask at least five people, such as family members, neighbors, and friends, to state the number of brothers and sisters or pets they have. Have students to draw a line plot for the data and then determine the mode.

Terrific T's Glyph

Directions: Follow the legend to design your T-shirt.

Terrific T's Legend

	Buttons: The number of buttons shows the number of brothers and sisters you have. Yellow buttons stand for sisters, and blue buttons stand for brothers.
	Stripes: One stripe across the bottom of the T-shirt means you like sports. One stripe across the edge of each sleeve means you like to read.
	Stars: An orange star on the left sleeve means pizza is your favorite food. A purple star on the right sleeve means hamburgers are your favorite food. A red star on both sleeves means your favorite food is something other than pizza or hamburgers.
	Triangles: The number of triangles across the bottom of the T-shirt shows your age. Color your triangles red if you are a girl. Color your triangles green if you are a boy.
	Collar: The color of the collar describes how many letters are in your first name. Color the collar yellow if your first name has six or fewer letters. Color it blue if your name has seven or more letters.

OUR FAVORITE THINGS

Objective

Students will learn to make a bar graph and read data.

Anticipatory Set

Assign the four corners of the classroom numbers from 1 to 4. Tell students they will participate in a short activity called Our Favorite Things. For the first round, tell students to stand in corner 1 if their favorite sport is baseball or softball. Tell them to stand in corner 2 if their favorite sport is basketball. Have them stand in corner 3 if their favorite sport is soccer or in corner 4 if their favorite sport is football.

Purpose

Tell students that they will be collecting data about their favorite things. They will make bar graphs to compare the data.

Input

Have students in each corner count how many are in their groups. Draw a bar graph on the overhead projector or the board to represent the number of students in each corner. Demonstrate how to label the side and the bottom of the graph as well as how to draw the bars.

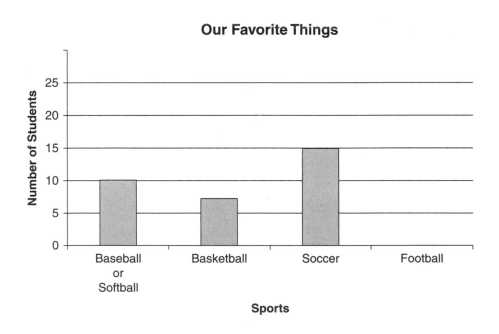

Play a second round of Our Favorite Things. Designate each corner as a favorite food, and ask students to stand in the corner of their choice. Have groups count the number of students in their corners. Then draw a bar graph to represent the data.

Modeling

Distribute graph paper for students to use to copy your work. On a transparency, model how to draw a bar graph to represent four favorite pets. Take a vote of students' favorite pets, and draw bars on the graph to represent the data.

Model another bar graph to represent four favorite ice cream flavors. Have students copy the graph. Take a vote of students' favorite flavors, and draw bars on the graph to represent the data.

Checking for Understanding

Walk through the classroom checking students' work to see if everyone understands how to draw a bar graph. Model more graphs as needed.

Guided Practice

Divide the class into groups of six or seven students. Direct each group to choose a topic for its favorite things graph, and limit the choices to four items. Ask each group to make its own bar graph for that topic. Instruct group members to vote for their favorite things and then poll other groups to vote for their favorite things. Have students collect the data and draw bars on their graphs to represent that data. Encourage group members to help each other make the graphs.

Closure

When students are finished, invite groups to share their graphs with the class. Prompt them to draw pictures of their bar graphs in their math journals. Have them write about what they learned during the activity.

Independent Practice

For homework, invite students to complete the **Out of This World reproducible (page 138).** The next day, gather students together to discuss their answers.

Extending the Activity

Host an ice cream party with at least four flavors of ice cream. When finished, make a large bar graph together on butcher paper to show how many students ate each flavor. Mount photographs of the party around the bar graph, and display it on a bulletin board.

Out of This World

The Out of This World Ice Cream Shop is holding a two-for-the-price-of-one ice cream party! All the aliens ordered their favorite flavor.

Directions: Look at the bar graph to answer the questions.

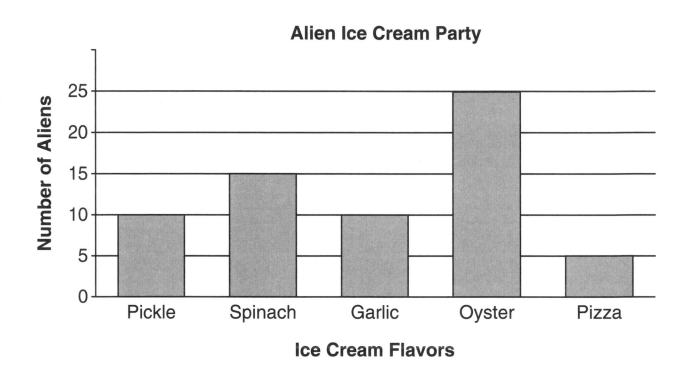

1. How many aliens got oyster ice cream? _____

2. How many aliens got garlic ice cream? _____

3. Which two flavors were eaten by the same number of aliens?_____

4. Which flavor did the aliens like the most? _____

5. Which flavor did the aliens like the least? _____

6. How many aliens got spinach ice cream? _____

BOOK BONANZA

Objective

Students will collect data and make a pictograph to represent those data.

Anticipatory Set

Using the **Project Reading reproducible (page 141)** as a guide, draw a pictograph on the board, but do not fill in any data. Label your pictograph "Our Favorite School Subjects." Prompt students to think of well-known symbols they see every day, such as symbols for the boys and girls bathrooms, no smoking signs, do-not-walk signs at traffic lights, and so on. Tell students that in this activity, they will use simple pictures or signs to represent data.

Purpose

Tell students that they have probably made pictographs in which each picture, or symbol, represents one person. Explain that they will learn how to make pictographs in which each picture represents more than one person. They will use the information on the graph to help them solve math problems.

> In a learning episode, we tend to remember best that which comes first and remember second best that which comes last.

Input

Ask four volunteers to share their favorite school subjects. Write the four subjects on the pictograph. Draw an apple below the graph, and point out that it represents two students. It should look like this: ⏾ = 2 students.

Invite students to vote for the subject from the list that they like best. Write the number on the board to the side of the chart. For example, if 11 students vote for one subject, ask, "Since one apple equals 2 students, how many apples should I draw on the graph?" (*five and one half*). Fill in the graph by drawing the corresponding number of apples to represent the data.

Using the Project Reading reproducible as a guide, show students how to solve math problems using the graph. For example, ask, "How many students voted for the first subject?" Count the apples together, and multiply by two to find the answer. Then ask, "How many more students voted for math than science?" First, count and multiply to determine the number of votes for each subject. Then, subtract to find the answer.

Modeling

Draw a new pictograph on the board. Have students copy your work onto a sheet of paper. Title your pictograph "Our Favorite Movies." This time, use a happy face rather than an apple for your pictograph. It should look like this: ☺ = 2 students.

Invite four new volunteers to name four favorite movies to list on the graph. Ask students to vote for their favorite movies. Write the numbers to the side of the graph. Choose a student to come to the board and draw the correct number of happy faces to represent the votes. Remind students that each happy face equals two students.

After the graph is complete, ask several questions about the data, such as, *Which movie did students vote for the most?* and *How many more students voted for the movie with the most votes than the movie with the least?* (Remind students to find the total votes for each movie and then subtract to find the answer.)

Checking for Understanding

Walk around the room, and look at students' work to check that everyone knows how to make a pictograph. Ask volunteers to explain their strategies for using the graph to solve math problems.

Guided Practice

Prompt students to make their own pictographs listing their four favorite books. Then have them walk around the room and ask at least 15 classmates to vote for their favorite books from the lists. After students collect the data, have them draw the corresponding number of objects (apples, happy faces, or any other objects they choose) on the graph to represent votes. Remind them that each object equals two students.

Ask students to solve several math problems using the graph, such as, *How many students voted for the book with the least number of votes?* and *How many more students voted for the first book than the second?*

Closure

Invite students to share their pictographs with the class. Prompt them to describe in their math journals the strategies they used to complete the activity.

Independent Practice

To provide more practice with pictographs, have students complete the Project Reading reproducible for homework.

Name_____ Date_____

Project Reading

The school library held a reading contest called Project Reading. At the end of the contest, students voted for their favorite books. The results are shown on the pictograph below.

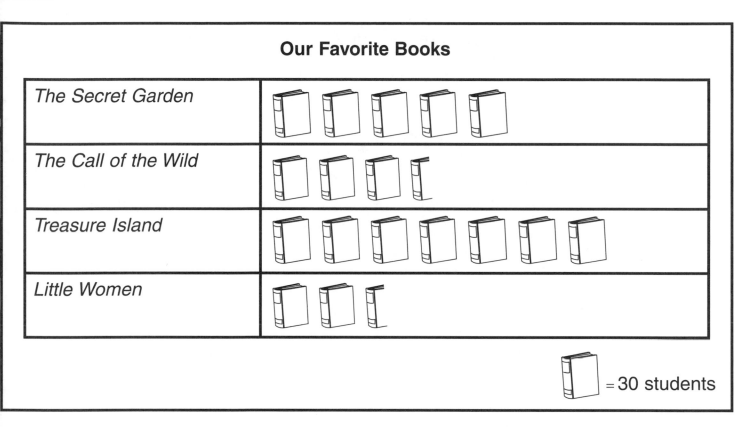

Directions: Use the pictograph to find the answers to these questions.

1. How many students voted for *The Call of the Wild?* _____

2. How many more students voted for *The Secret Garden* than *Little Women?* _____

3. Which book received 150 votes? _____

4. Which book did students vote for the most? _____

5. How many students voted for *Little Women?* _____

6. How many more students voted for *Treasure Island* than *The Call of the Wild?*_____

TOO MANY ANTS!

Objective

Students will learn how to identify coordinates and locate points on a grid.

Anticipatory Set

Place a transparency of half-inch grid paper on the overhead projector. Using the **(1,2) Bingo! Cards reproducible (page 144)** as a guide, draw a grid on the transparency. Label up the left side and across the bottom from 0 to 10.

Metaphors can help students establish meaning for new learning.

Then ask each student to imagine that a line of ants marched into his or her house. The grid is the floor of the house, and the ants are marching everywhere along the lines of the grid.

Purpose

Tell students that they need to find all the ants in the house. Explain that if they can collect the ants, they can use them to create an ant farm.

Input

Mark the point (4,2) on the grid. Point to the dot and say, "Look! We found an ant!" Before you can pick up the ant, however, students must name the point on the grid to describe the ant's location. Tell students, "To locate the point on the grid, begin at 0." Place your marker on the transparency at 0. "First, go *right* four units." Draw a horizontal line from 0 to 4. "Then, go *up* two units." Draw a vertical line from 4 to 2 to land on the point.

Write "(4,2)" on the transparency next to the dot. Explain that these numbers make up the *ordered pair* for this point. The numbers in an ordered pair are called *coordinates*. Tell students, "The first number in an ordered pair tells how many units the ant moved to the *right*. The second number in an ordered pair tells how many units the ant moved *up*. Together, an ordered pair shows that the ant moved *right up* to stop on that point on the grid."

Modeling

For this activity, students will write the ordered pair for each point you draw on the grid. When you say, "buddy check," students show the coordinates to a partner. Both partners must agree on the answer. You will call on volunteers to write the ordered pairs on the transparency.

Mark the point (6,5) on the grid and say, "This ant moved *right up* to this point on the grid." Instruct students to write the ordered pair. Say, "buddy check," and allow time for students to check their answers with partners. Invite a volunteer to write the coordinates on the transparency. Model several more examples on the grid.

Checking for Understanding

Ask students if they understand each step of the activity. Invite volunteers to explain how to locate a point on a grid.

Guided Practice

Make several copies of the (1,2) Bingo! Cards reproducible. Cut out the cards, and give each student one Bingo card. (If you wish, make a variety of Bingo cards for the game so not so many students have the same cards.)

How to Play the Game

To begin, draw a blank grid on graph paper that resembles those on the Bingo cards. Then choose and mark a random point on your grid. Write the ordered pair, and call it out for students. Allow time for students to look at their grids. If that point is marked on their grids, they write the ordered pair on scrap paper. (They will *not* write on the grid.) If that point is not marked, students simply wait until the next ordered pair is called.

Mark another random point on your grid. Write the ordered pair below the first, and call it out for students. Again, allow time for students to look at their grids. If that point is marked, they write the ordered pair. Continue choosing random points, writing them on your grid and calling out the ordered pairs.

When students have five ordered pairs, they should shout, "Bingo!" The first students who write five ordered pairs win that round of the game. Have students check their answers against your grid to make sure they marked the correct ordered pairs. Then ask students to exchange Bingo cards and play the game again. Be sure to draw a new blank grid.

Closure

Ask students to draw grids in their math journals and mark five ants or points on them. Have them write the corresponding coordinates. Ask them to reflect on how using the idea of ants in the activity helped them learn the concept.

Independent Practice

For homework, have students complete the **Ants, Ants, Ants! reproducible (page 145).** Remind them to go *right up* to find the points on the grid.

(1,2) Bingo! Cards

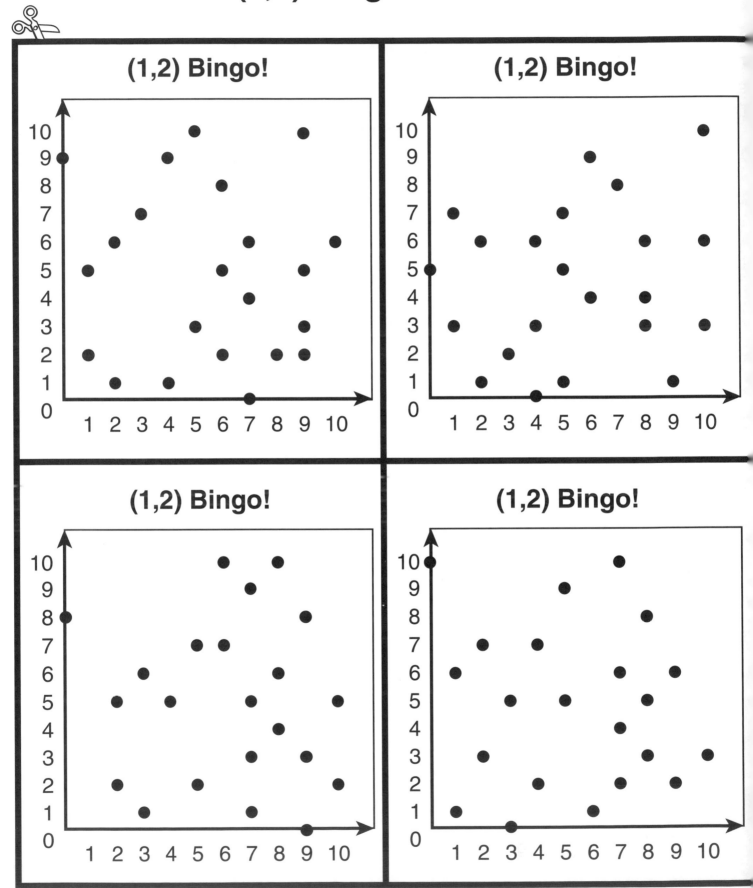

Ants, Ants, Ants!

Directions: Ants are in the store! Ants are in the school! Ants are at the park! Ants are everywhere! Use the grid to help you find all the ants.

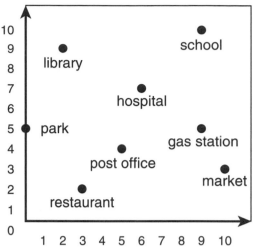

1. Name the place where you found these ants. Begin at 0. Go right 3. Go up 2. _____

2. Name the place where you found these ants. Begin at 0. Go right 9. Go up 10. _____

3. These ants are reading books at the library. Write the ordered pair for that point.

_____

4. These ants are playing at the park. Write the ordered pair for that point. _____

5. These ants are opening the mail! Write the ordered pair for that point. _____

6. Describe how to find the ants at the market.

   Begin at _____. Go right _____. Go up _____.

7. Describe how to find the ants at the hospital.

   Begin at _____. Go right _____. Go up _____.

8. Describe how to find the ants at the gas station.

   Begin at _____. Go right _____. Go up _____.

145

SURVEY STUDY

Objective

Students will conduct a survey and make graphs to display and interpret their results.

Anticipatory Set

Display examples of tally charts, pictographs, bar graphs, histograms, line graphs, and circle graphs from sources such as business newspapers, web sites, sales brochures, and math textbooks. (You might also ask students to collect and bring in their own samples.) Ask students, "Where might you see examples of graphs like these in real life? Why do you think graphs are used to show data, such as for an election or for a business project?"

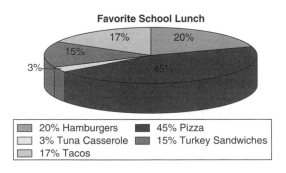

Favorite School Lunch

- 20% Hamburgers
- 3% Tuna Casserole
- 17% Tacos
- 45% Pizza
- 15% Turkey Sandwiches

Purpose

Explain to students that *data* are a collection of numbers often organized in graphs or charts. These graphs and charts present data in a way that helps people understand them. Different types of graphs and charts can be used, depending on the data being presented. In this activity, students will conduct their own survey and show their results using three types of graphic representations.

Input

Review with students the parts of a tally chart, pictograph, bar graph, histogram, line graph, and circle graph. Display examples as you explain and compare the different parts of each graph. Clarify how and when to use each type of graph to represent data.

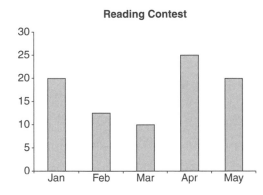

Reading Contest

Pictograph: This graph shows rows of identical picture symbols (with a picture key) to represent multiple numbers, such as one apple for every 10 votes.

Bar Graph: This graph shows rectangular bars drawn either vertically or horizontally along a number scale of equal intervals to represent categories of data. A bar graph is a good choice when you want to make comparisons between data. The bars should be drawn with equal width (to prevent distorting or misrepresenting results), and there should be equal space between bars. A double bar graph can be used to compare two data sets, such as boys and girls surveyed separately about favorite pets.

Histogram: This special kind of bar graph displays the frequency of data within equal intervals, such as within specific age ranges. There are no spaces between bars.

Line Graph: On a line graph, data are plotted like ordered pairs on a number grid. The points are then connected to show change over time, such as changes in temperature or fluctuating stock prices. A double line graph (or multiple line graph) can be used to compare two (or more) data sets, such as January temperatures for two states.

Circle Graph (Pie Graph): This graph consists of a circle divided into sections that represent parts of a data set. A different-colored section usually represents each data category. The size of each section is determined by the percentage of the total amount. For example, one quarter of a circle is blue to represent 25 percent of pet owners surveyed who own cats.

Modeling

Take a quick poll of students about favorite pets. Provide four choices, such as dog, cat, fish, and bird. Tally the results separately for boys and girls. Then demonstrate how to display the results as a pictograph, single bar graph (all students), and double bar graph (comparing boys and girls). Have students help decide the appropriate key and number scale to use for each graph. Point out that the number scale starts at zero and consists of equally spaced and numbered increments.

Demonstrate how data on a graph can be distorted or misleading. For example, draw a short bar much wider than a tall bar to make it look like more, or use small increments (e.g., counting by twos instead of tens) to stretch out a smaller amount.

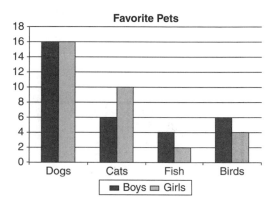

Guided Practice

With your guidance, invite students to draw their own circle graphs of the class survey. First, calculate the percentage of total votes for each category. Then, multiply the amount by 360° to determine the size of the section to color for that category. Next, use a protractor to draw that section on the circle. Show how to round off any partial percentages and degrees to the nearest whole number, and check that all categories add up to a total of 100% and 360°:

Category	Votes (Boys & Girls)	% Total Votes	Degrees of a Circle
Dogs	8 + 8 = 16 for dogs	$^{16}/_{32}$ = 50%	0.5 × 360° = 180°
Cats	3 + 5 = 8 for cats	$^{8}/_{32}$ = 25%	0.25 × 360° = 90°
Fish	2 + 1 = 3 for fish	$^{3}/_{32}$ = 9%	0.09 × 360° = 32.4°
Birds	3 + 2 = 5 for birds	$^{5}/_{32}$ = 16%	0.16 × 360° = 57.6°

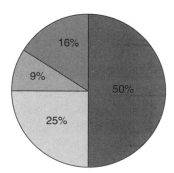

50% (or 180°) Dogs
25% (or 90°) Cats
9% (or 32.4°) Fish
16% (or 57.6°) Birds

Checking for Understanding

Check that students understand the different ways to graph data and interpret results. Ask questions such as, *Which pet does our class like the most? The*

least? Which type of graph do you think works best for these data? Why? How are the graphs alike? and *How are they different?*

Independent Practice

Have students conduct their own survey and make a poster showing their results. They should include a tally chart, their choice of three graphic representations, and at least three math questions (and answers) that analyze, compare, and interpret the results. Help them get started by brainstorming together a list of possible topics. Tell students that they must survey at least 30 people and offer at least four choices. Allow several days to complete the assignment, checking students' progress daily. You might encourage students to use computer technology to organize and graph their data.

Closure

Display the completed posters, and have students share and compare their results. Ask the class to solve the math problems written for each survey. Then encourage students to answer the following questions in their math journals: "What did you learn about conducting surveys, showing data, and interpreting results? What helped you complete this activity successfully? What math and organizational skills did you use?"

FAST FOOD COMPARISONS

Objective

Students will find the mean, median, mode, and range of calories for different groups of fast foods and analyze the results.

Anticipatory Set

Ask students to raise their hands if they have eaten at a fast food restaurant. Invite students to share their thoughts about whether they think fast foods are healthy. Then ask them to share what they know about calories. Ask, "How many calories do you think you must consume each day to stay healthy? How many calories do you think are in a hamburger? How many calories do you think are in a fast food meal?" Share the following examples with your students:

Hamburger = 280 calories

Small fries = 270 calories

Small soda = 160 calories

Purpose

Explain to students that *calories* are the energy we get from consuming food and beverages. It is important for a healthy body to consume enough calories each day to obtain the energy needed to function properly. However, too many calories can lead to weight gain and other possible health problems. In this activity, students will compare the calories of some popular fast foods and draw conclusions based on the data.

Input

Explain to students that the mean, median, and mode are measures of central tendency used to analyze and compare data. Have students write the following definitions and examples in their math journals as you explain and compare the information. (Point out that for this example, the large range means that the values are spread out, which could lead to a notable disparity between the mean and the median.)

- The *mean* is the average value of a data set, calculated by adding all the values and then dividing by the total number of values (addends) in the set.
- The *median* is the middle value of the data set in numerical order. If there is an even number of values, the median is determined by adding the two middle values and dividing by two (finding the average of the two middle values).

- The *mode* is the value that occurs most often in the set (the value with the greatest frequency). There can be more than one mode or no mode at all.
- The *range* is the span of numbers in the data set, which is the difference between the greatest and least values.

Example

Data: 265, 342, 189, 227, 445, 200

Ordered least to greatest: 189, 200, 227, 265, 342, 445

Mean: $(189 + 200 + 227 + 265 + 342 + 445) \div 6$ values $= 1{,}668 \div 6 = 278$

Median: For an even number of values $= (227 + 265) \div 2 = 246$

Mode: None (all values occur only once)

Range: $445 - 189 = 256$

Modeling

Display the **Fast Food Chart 1 reproducible (page 153).** Point out that the top chart shows the calories for hamburgers at five restaurants. If students find the measures of central tendency, they can better analyze and compare the data.

Demonstrate how to order the values for the first five hamburgers (regular hamburgers) from least to greatest and find the median (middle value), mode (greatest frequency), mean (sum of values ÷ number of values), and range (greatest value – lowest value).

Regular Hamburgers

Order = 250, 270, 280, 280, 320   **Mean** = $1{,}400 \div 5 = 280$

Median = 280   **Range** = $320 - 250 = 70$

Mode = 280

Analyze the results, asking questions such as, *Which regular hamburger has the most calories? The least calories? What is the range of calories for these hamburgers?* and *About how many calories is the average regular hamburger?* Point out that all three measures of central tendency are the same for this set (280 cal).

Then show how to find the median, mode, mean, and range for the other five hamburgers (specialty hamburgers). Analyze the results accordingly.

Specialty Hamburgers

Order = 410, 550, 590, 590, 680   **Mean** = $2{,}820 \div 5 = 564$

Median = 590   **Range** = $680 - 410 = 270$

Mode = 590

Point out that the range for the specialty hamburgers is greater than for the regular hamburgers due to the top and bottom values (*outliers*), which affects the value for the mean.

Invite students to predict the central tendencies for all 10 hamburgers. Encourage them to consider the previous results as well as the increasing range of calories. Then calculate and show the results, noting the even number of values in the data set (10):

Regular and Specialty Hamburgers

Order = 250, 270, 280, 280, 320, 410, 550, 590, 590, 680

Median = (320 + 410) ÷ 2 = 365

Modes = 280 and 590

Mean = 4,220 ÷ 10 = 422

Range = 680 − 250 = 430

Compare and analyze the results, pointing out the two modes (both with a double frequency), the large range, and the difference between the median and the mean.

> Explore every opportunity for students to see the practical applications of mathematics. Whenever possible, ask students to graph, compare, predict, and discuss their data and measurements.

Guided Practice

Give students calculators and copies of the **Fast Food Chart 1, Fast Food Chart 2,** and **Fast Food Comparisons reproducibles (pages 153–157).** Have them fill in the answers for the median, mode, mean, and range for the hamburger data. Then assign student groups to work cooperatively to complete the rest of part 1. Groups can divide the work and then share their results. Ask students to show their work on scratch paper or in their math journals.

Review the answers to part 1 before continuing on to part 2, having groups read aloud their answers to compare with other groups. Complete the answers for the first hamburger meal deal together, showing students how to refer to part 1 to find the calories for each item. Decide together which measure of central tendency to use for each item.

Then have groups work together to complete the second problem. Check their answers before having them continue on to problems 3 and 4. Group members may decide individually which extra items to include for each meal.

Checking for Understanding

Call on students to share their answers for problem 4, along with observations and conclusions about the results. Ask, "Which measure of central tendency did you use for the calories of each item in the meal deal? Why? What do you notice about the differences in total calories for the regular meals and the specialty meals? Between the hamburger meals and the chicken meals? What do you notice about adding the extras?"

Independent Practice

Review the directions for part 3, and answer any questions. Ask students to complete this page as a homework assignment. Remind them to refer to the results from parts 1 and 2. They should use their own ages for the calories needed per day and per meal (total calories divided by three for three equal meals).

Closure

Invite students to share their results from part 3 and summarize what they learned in their math journals. Ask, "What conclusions can you draw from the results? How did your math skills help you analyze and compare the data?"

Extending the Activity

- Suggest that students make a line plot of fast food data and then find the median, mode, mean, and range. First, use data from the Fast Food Charts to show students how to make a line plot. Then have them go online (www.fastfood.com/nutrition or www.foodfacts.info) to collect more data to organize, plot, and find the measures of central tendency.
- Explain to students that exercising regularly helps them burn calories and keep their bodies healthy. Ask them to go online to research the approximate number of calories they will burn per hour for each of these activities (the number burned depends on body weight): basketball, bicycle riding, jogging, jumping rope, swimming laps, and walking.
- Have students use online sources to compare the nutritional value (grams of fat, protein, and so on) of fast foods, or compare the local prices of those foods. You might also ask them to compare the nutritional values of fast foods to fresh foods prepared at home.

Fast Food Chart 1

Regular Hamburgers	Calories*
Burger King Hamburger	320
Carl's Jr. Hamburger	280
Jack in the Box Hamburger	250
McDonald's Hamburger	280
Wendy's Hamburger (Junior)	270
Specialty Hamburgers	
Burger King Whopper	680
Carl's Jr. Famous Star	590
Jack in the Box Jumbo Jack	550
McDonald's Big Mac	590
Wendy's Classic Single With Everything	410

***Extra per serving (approximate):** Cheese +100 cal; Catsup +10 cal; Mustard +20 cal; Mayonnaise +100 cal; Specialty Sauces (barbecue, sweet and sour) +80 cal.

Chicken Sandwiches	Calories*
Burger King Broiler Chicken Sandwich	550
Carl's Jr. Charbroiled Chicken Sandwich	290
Jack in the Box Chicken Sandwich	400
McDonald's Chicken McGrill Sandwich	450
Wendy's Grilled Chicken Sandwich	300
Chicken Club Sandwiches	
Burger King Chicken Club Sandwich	740
Carl's Jr. Charbroiled Chicken Club Sandwich	470
Jack in the Box Grilled Chicken Club Sandwich	520
McDonald's Crispy Chicken Club Sandwich	550
Wendy's Chicken Club Sandwich	470

***Extra per serving (approximate):** Cheese +100 cal; Catsup +10 cal; Mustard +20 cal; Mayonnaise +100 cal; Specialty Sauces (barbecue, sweet and sour) +80 cal.

Fast Food Chart 2

French Fries	Calories*
Burger King French Fries (small)	230
Carl's Jr. French Fries (small)	290
Jack in the Box French Fries (small)	350
McDonald's French Fries (small)	210
Wendy's French Fries (small)	270
Burger King French Fries (large)	600
Carl's Jr. French Fries (large)	620
Jack in the Box French Fries (large)	610
McDonald's French Fries (large)	610
Wendy's French Fries (large)	570

Extra per serving (approximate): Cheese +100 cal; Catsup +10 cal; Mustard +20 cal; Mayonnaise +100 cal; Specialty Sauces (barbecue, sweet and sour) +80 cal.

Garden Salads (no dressing)	Calories*
Jack in the Box Side Garden Salad	50
McDonald's Garden Salad	100
Wendy's Deluxe Garden Salad	110
Chicken Salads (no dressing)	
Jack in the Box Chicken Salad	200
McDonald's Grilled Chicken Caesar Salad	100
Wendy's Grilled Chicken Salad	200

Extra per serving (approximate) for salad dressing: Caesar +300 cal; Italian +100 cal; Thousand Island +250 cal; Ranch +200 cal; Reduced Calorie Dressing $= \frac{1}{3}$ of calories.

Drinks	Calories
Coca Cola (small, medium, large)	160, 230, 330
Sprite (small, medium, large)	160, 220, 320
Dr. Pepper (small, medium, large)	160, 220, 320

Fast Food Comparisons: Part 1

Directions: Use the Fast Food Charts to find the median, mode, mean, and range of calories for each data set.

Fast Foods	Median	Mode	Mean	Range
1. Regular Hamburgers				
2. Specialty Hamburgers				
3. Regular Chicken				
4. Chicken Club				
5. Small Fries				
6. Large Fries				
7. Garden Salads				
8. Chicken Salads				
9. Small Drinks				
10. Medium Drinks				
11. Large Drinks				

Fast Food Comparisons: Part 2

Directions: Use your results from Fast Food Comparisons: Part 1 to estimate the total calories for each "meal deal."

1. Regular Hamburger Meal = regular hamburger, small fries, small drink

    _____ cal + _____ cal + _____ cal = _____ Total Calories

2. Specialty Hamburger Meal = specialty hamburger, large fries, large drink

    _____ cal + _____ cal + _____ cal = _____ Total Calories

3. Regular Chicken Meal = regular chicken sandwich, small fries, small drink

    _____ cal + _____ cal + _____ cal = _____ Total Calories

4. Chicken Club Meal = chicken club sandwich, large fries, large drink

    _____ cal + _____ cal + _____ cal = _____ Total Calories

Directions: Look at the "extras per serving" listed below each food chart. Which of these extras do you put on your food? Add those calories to each total.

5. Regular Hamburger Meal =

    _____ cal + _____ extra cal = _____ Total Calories

6. Specialty Hamburger Meal =

    _____ cal + _____ extra cal = _____ Total Calories

7. Regular Chicken Meal =

    _____ cal + _____ extra cal = _____ Total Calories

8. Chicken Club Meal =

    _____ cal + _____ extra cal = _____ Total Calories

9. What do you notice about the above results? On the back of this paper, write at least three comparisons.

Fast Food Comparisons: Part 3

Directions: Complete the chart below. The Adults section is done for you.

Approximate Calories (Energy) Needed

Age	Total Calories per Day		Calories per Meal ($\frac{1}{3}$ of Total)	
	Boys	Girls	Boys	Girls
7–10	1,970	1,740		
11–14	2,220	1,850		
15–18	2,760	2,110		
Adults	2,550	1,940	2,550 ÷ 3 = 850 cal	1,940 ÷ 3 = 647 cal

Directions: Compare the calories needed (above) to the calories of each "meal deal" from Part 2.

Regular Hamburger Meal

Calories of meal deal (with extras) = _____

How many more or fewer calories do you need per meal? _____

Percent of total daily calories: (meal deal ÷ your total daily calories) × 100 = _____ %

Specialty Hamburger Meal

Calories of meal deal (with extras) = _____

How many more or fewer calories do you need per meal? _____

Percent of total daily calories: (meal deal ÷ your total daily calories) × 100 = _____ %

Regular Chicken Meal

Calories of meal deal (with extras) = _____

How many more or fewer calories do you need per meal? _____

Percent of total daily calories: (meal deal ÷ your total daily calories) × 100 = _____ %

Chicken Club Meal

Calories of meal deal (with extras) = _____

How many more or fewer calories do you need per meal? _____

Percent of total daily calories: (meal deal ÷ your total daily calories) × 100 = _____ %

What conclusions can you draw about these results? What might be a healthy alternative for a meal? Write your conclusions and ideas in your math journal.

PARACHUTE DROP

Objectives

Students will make, test, and graph the results of different sizes and shapes of parachutes.

Students will draw conclusions about the relationship between parachute area and speed of descent.

Anticipatory Set

Set up workstations in the classroom that include the following materials: plastic trash bags or tissue paper, scissors, rulers, calculators, string, unsharpened pencils or markers, tape, stopwatches, and graph paper.

Show students pictures of people jumping with parachutes, and ask, "What do you know about parachutes? Do you know anyone who has gone skydiving? Describe their experiences. What affects how fast they drop? What math skills do you think are involved in making and testing a parachute?" Have students record their ideas in their math journals.

> When teachers encourage students to invent alternative problem-solving strategies, the learning objectives are different from those that result from instruction using standard memorization procedures. The emphasis is on making sense and finding meaning in the methods that students create and successfully use.

Purpose

Explain to students that parachutes come in many different sizes and shapes and are made from many different types of materials. However, all parachutes have one purpose—to catch air and slow the attached person or object for a safe, smooth landing. In this activity, students will make and test six sizes and shapes of parachutes and graph the results to see if there is a relationship between a parachute's area and drop time.

Input

Tell students that a parachute works by creating drag (added air resistance), which slows the person or object attached to it for a gentle landing. Point out that on windy days, there is more air resistance, requiring more weight to counteract it.

Review with students how to calculate the area of a square ($A = s^2$) and a triangle ($A = \frac{1}{2} bh$). They will need to know how to calculate the area of squares and triangles for their parachutes:

- Square has 12-in/cm sides ($A = 12 \times 12 = 144$ in²/cm²).
- Triangle has a 12-in/cm base and a 6-in/cm height ($A = \frac{1}{2}[12 \times 6] = 36$ in²/cm²).

Modeling

Show students how to make a square parachute, as described on the **Parachute Drop: Part 1 reproducible (page 161).** Cut a large square from a plastic bag. Measure the length, and calculate the area. Then cut four 6-in strings, and tape one to each of the square's four corners. Tie the loose ends of the strings to a pencil to represent an attached person.

Ask a student to help you demonstrate how to test the parachute. Drop it from a specific height, and time how long it takes for the parachute to land on the ground from the moment of release. Write the time on the board under "Test 1." Then repeat the process, pointing out the importance of dropping the parachute from exactly the same height for consistency. Record the second time under "Test 2." Show students how to find the average by adding the two times and then dividing by two.

Explain to students that they will make a graph comparing the area of each parachute to its average drop time. Demonstrate how to set up the graph, with "Parachute Area" along the horizontal axis and "Drop Time" along the vertical axis. Plot the data for the parachute you just tested. Tell students that their graph will include a total of six points.

Guided Practice

Give students copies of the **Parachute Drop reproducibles (pages 161–162).** Divide the class into groups of three to work at each station. Have each group make six parachutes according to the directions. Monitor students' progress, and make sure students are measuring correctly. Remind them to refer to your example.

After all groups have completed their six parachutes, have them test their parachutes outdoors or in an indoor area such as the school gym. Before they begin, demonstrate again how to test each parachute twice, reminding them to drop their parachutes from the same height. (You might have students stand safely on a chair to drop parachutes, or they can drop parachutes from the second floor of a building with school permission.) Encourage students to predict how long it will take for each parachute to land on the ground based on previous results, and then compare their predictions to the actual results.

After students have tested all of their parachutes and recorded the data, take them back to the classroom. Have them complete their graphs and answer the questions about their results. Circulate around the room, and monitor their progress. Refer students to the sample graph on the board, and help them graph their data correctly as needed.

Checking for Understanding

Invite each group to share its results and conclusions, including its answers to the questions on the reproducible. Check that students have measured, recorded, and interpreted their results correctly. Discuss any differences among the groups' results.

Independent Practice

Have each group write its data (six parachute areas and drop times) on the board for the rest of the students to copy into their math journals. For homework, have each student use the data to make a class version of the Parachute Area versus Drop Time graph and then compare that graph to his or her own group's graph. The next day, gather students together for a discussion. Ask, "How are the class results similar to your own group's results? Which factors could have influenced the results?"

Closure

Invite students to summarize in their math journals what they learned from this activity and explain how they used their math skills. Prompt them with questions such as, *How did you use the area of parachutes for this activity? How did you collect, organize, and interpret your data? What conclusions did you make about the area of a parachute and the time it takes for the parachute to land? How could you use your results to predict the time for another parachute to drop?* and *How might this information be helpful in other areas of your life?*

Extending the Activity

- Suggest that students calculate the mean, median, mode, and range of their data results.
- Invite students to test and make graphs showing how changing the weight (tying on increasing numbers of pencils), string length, or parachute shape (testing other polygons) affects the results. You might also have them measure the distance each parachute lands from an intended target and explore ways to improve accuracy. Challenge students to create a parachute with a slow drop rate and a precise landing.
- Ask teams to conduct similar testing for paper airplanes, graphing distance versus surface area of the wings.

Name_____   Date_____

Parachute Drop: Part 1

Directions: Work with two other classmates. Follow the steps below to make and compare six different parachutes.

You Will Need:

- plastic trash bags or tissue paper
- scissors
- ruler
- calculator
- string

- tape
- unsharpened pencils or markers
- stopwatch
- graph paper
- math journal or scratch paper

---

1. Cut out three squares of different sizes (small, medium, large) from a plastic bag or tissue paper. Fold the squares in half, and trim off any extra to make sure they are perfect squares.

2. Cut out three isosceles triangles of different sizes (small, medium, large) from a plastic bag or tissue paper. Fold the triangles in half, and trim off any extra to make sure they are perfect isosceles triangles (two sides congruent).

3. Use a ruler and calculator to determine the area of each parachute in inches, using the formula for a square ($A = s^2$) or a triangle ($A = \frac{1}{2} bh$). Record the data below.

Square Parachutes: Area

Small:_____

Medium:_____

Large:_____

Triangle Parachutes: Area

Small:_____

Medium:_____

Large:_____

4. Cut 21 six-inch pieces of string (four per square, three per triangle). Tape the end of a piece of string to the corners of each parachute. Then tie an unsharpened pencil or marker to the other ends of the strings to represent a person or object.

Parachute Drop: Part 2

Directions: Now test your parachutes one at a time:

- Student 1 drops each parachute from the exact same place and height.
- Student 2 times the parachute's descent from the moment of release to the time it hits the ground.
- Student 3 records the results for each drop.
- Repeat the test twice for each parachute. Then calculate the average.

Square Parachutes: Drop Times

	Test 1	Test 2	Average Time (Sum ÷ 2)
Small			
Medium			
Large			

Triangle Parachutes: Drop Times

	Test 1	Test 2	Average Time (Sum ÷ 2)
Small			
Medium			
Large			

Parachute Drop: Part 3

Directions: Use graph paper to make a line graph of your results, plotting parachute area versus drop time. Along the horizontal axis, use square inches labeled *Parachute Area.* Along the vertical axis, use seconds labeled *Drop Time.* Plot the average time for each parachute. Use a different color for squares and triangles.

What do your results show? Answer these questions on another sheet of paper.

1. Which parachute performed the best? The worst? Why do you think so?

2. Is there a relationship between the area of the parachute and drop time? Does a greater area equal a longer drop time? Explain.

3. Does the shape of the parachute make a difference? Why do you think so?

PLOT THE TREASURE

Objective

Students will use ordered pairs on a coordinate grid to plot and identify the locations of hidden objects.

Anticipatory Set

Display a road map or other kind of map drawn on a coordinate grid. Ask students, "Suppose I want you to find a specific place or object on this map. How can I tell you where to find it without naming or describing it?"

Purpose

Tell students that they can use *ordered pairs* on a *coordinate grid* to identify the locations of places and objects on a map. In this activity, students will use a coordinate grid to map out and locate a hidden treasure.

> Look for opportunities to present and solve problems outdoors or in a large indoor area like the gymnasium. Movement and greater social interaction stimulate long-term memory and create interest in the lesson.

Input

On the overhead projector, show and explain the parts of a coordinate grid. (You may use the **Plot the Treasure reproducible [page 166]** copied onto a transparency.) Label and number all the parts of the grid as you proceed with the lesson. Point out the number line along the horizontal axis (x-axis) and the vertical axis (y-axis), as well as the *center of origin*. Tell students that they can use ordered pairs to indicate specific locations on the grid and draw dots to show these locations.

Write an example of an ordered pair, such as (3,5). Explain that the first number tells how many places to move along the horizontal axis (side to side), whereas the second number tells how many places to move along the vertical axis (up and down). As a helpful hint, tell students to always move "flat first" (horizontally first).

Explain how to plot both positive and negative numbers on your coordinate grid: quad I (+,+), quad II (−,+), quad III (−,−), quad IV (+,−). For positive x values (horizontal axis), you move to the right. For negative values, you move to the left. Similarly, for positive y values, you move upward. For negative values, you move downward. Using the coordinate grid, demonstrate the differences between the locations of these ordered pairs: (3,5), (−3,5), (−3,−5), (3,−5).

Modeling

Tell students that they will draw an aerial view (map) of their school on a coordinate grid. They will then use ordered pairs from the grid map to find hidden clues for a treasure hunt.

Demonstrate by drawing an aerial view of your classroom on the transparency coordinate grid. Draw simple shapes (squares, rectangles, circles) for the main objects in the room, including student desks. Label the objects "window," "door," "teacher's desk," and so on. Then write the ordered pairs for the locations of people or objects at specific places in the room. For example, write the ordered pair for the location of your desk, such as (2,8), and draw a large dot on that spot on the grid map. Repeat the process several times.

Checking for Understanding

Call out ordered pairs, and have students identify the person or object located at that spot on the grid map. Ask questions such as, *According to this map, who is sitting at point (5,4)?* Invite students to help you plot each point on the grid map. Repeat several times. Leave the grid map on display for students to refer to as they make their own maps.

Guided Practice

Give each student a copy of the Plot the Treasure reproducible. Have students work in pairs to draw aerial views of the school on the coordinate grid and use ordered pairs to pinpoint the locations of hidden clues for a treasure hunt.

First, have students label the coordinate grid using positive and negative whole numbers. Then, direct them to draw simple shapes to represent each building and area of the school. Assist as needed. Tell students to draw relative sizes, for example, a larger rectangle for the cafeteria than for their classroom. Remind them not to label or color any parts since they should be relying on ordered pairs to navigate around the school.

Suggest that students write at least eight clues (ordered pairs) to hide around the school, and label them "clue 1," "clue 2," "clue 3," and so on. Each clue should include an ordered pair that directs someone to the next clue, in sequence. Each clue should also provide a hint (cryptic or rhyming message) telling where to look, for example, "Clue 1: Go to (3,4). Look behind the building door!"

Have students make two copies of their lists—one to use as an answer key and one to cut apart and hide for the treasure hunt. On the answer key, make sure they include the correct location for each clue. For example, "Clue 1: Go to (3,4). Look behind the building door! (Answer: library door)."

Before students hide their clues, have them draw (or stamp) a unique, identical symbol on each clue so searchers can confirm that they have found a clue for the correct treasure hunt (in case more than one pair hides clues in the same area). To keep all treasure hunt materials organized, have students stamp their answer keys and grid maps with the same symbols.

Allow students plenty of time to hide their clues for the treasure hunt. Emphasize that all locations must be safe areas and easily accessible. At the last location, students should hide a small treasure (e.g., stickers, pencils, small treats).

Before students begin their treasure hunt, collect all the first clues, grid maps, and answer keys. Then pass out matching grid maps and first clues to random student pairs. Remind pairs to use the grid maps to locate the places indicated by the ordered pair on each clue. Direct them to keep all of their clues, not discard them, since they will need them later.

If a student pair cannot find a clue within 5 minutes, instruct the students to come to you for the answer so they can continue the search. After pairs find the hidden treasure, have them return to their desks and glue the clues in sequence on a sheet of paper. Invite students to summarize in their math journals how they used ordered pairs and the grid map to find the hidden treasure.

Closure

When everyone has found his or her treasure and is seated back in the classroom, initiate a class discussion about the treasure hunt. Ask students to share their experiences making a treasure map and using clues to navigate around the school grounds. Prompt them with questions such as, *What are the parts of a coordinate grid? What are ordered pairs? How do you use ordered pairs to plot or identify points on a coordinate grid?* and *How did you use this knowledge to help you make and use a grid map for the treasure hunt?*

Independent Practice

For homework, have each student draw an aerial view of his or her bedroom or house on a coordinate grid and use ordered pairs to identify the locations of different places or objects. Suggest that students write creative stories about trying to find a lost object, using ordered pairs to name the locations of different places they searched around their rooms or houses before finding it.

Plot the Treasure

Directions: Use the coordinate grid to draw an aerial map (top view) of your school. Use simple shapes to show the locations of different buildings and areas. On another sheet of paper, write clues for a treasure hunt by using ordered pairs from this map.

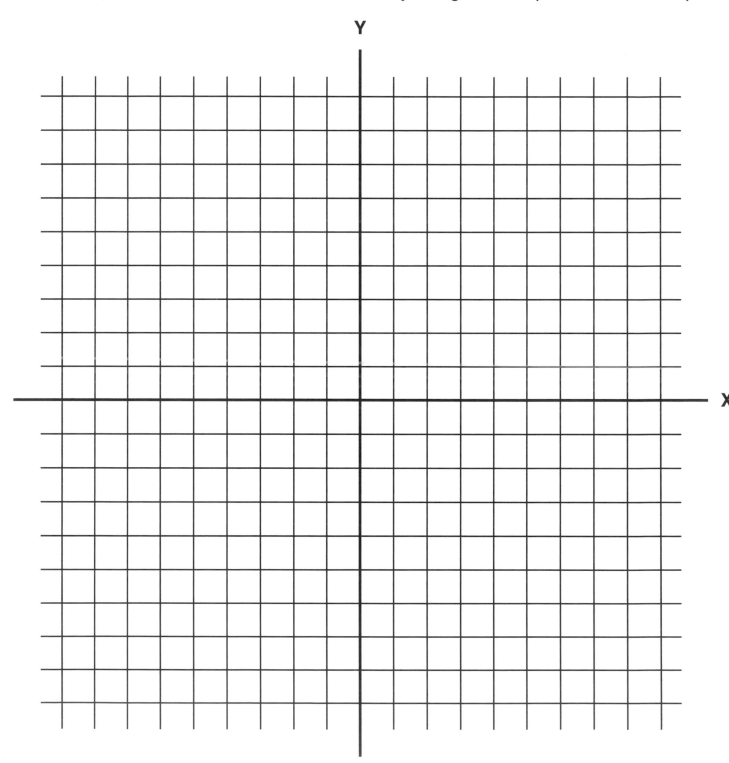

ANIMAL OLYMPICS

Objective

Students will organize, graph, and interpret data about athletic animals and themselves.

Anticipatory Set

Display pictures of several types of animals on the board, such as a frog, a cheetah, an elephant, and a kangaroo. Ask students, "If these animals could participate in the Olympics, in which events do you think they would perform best?" (*Possible answers: frog—long jump, cheetah—100-meter dash, elephant— weight lifting, kangaroo—high jump*). "What kind of data do you think we are going to explore today? What math skills do you think are involved with athletic events?"

Purpose

Explain to students that athletic competitions, such as the Olympics, involve comparing speed, distance, and endurance of the competitors. In this activity, students will explore data of some impressive athletic animals and then test their own relay abilities.

> Vary your lesson delivery style during each class period to appeal to different learning styles. Remember that all students benefit when they use a variety of modalities while learning.

Input

On the board, write, "Cheetah: 70 mph (113 km/hr)." Explain to students that *mph* stands for "miles per hour," and a cheetah can run 70 mph (usually only for short distances). For comparison, a car moves at about 55 mph (88.51 km/hr) on the freeway, which means that a cheetah can outrun a car traveling at that speed.

Show students that by dividing 70 mph (113 km/hr) by 60 min (or 1 hr), you can calculate how far a cheetah can run per minute: $70 \div 60 =$ about 1.2 miles, or about $1\frac{1}{5}$ miles (113 km/hr $\div$ 60 = 1.88 km). For comparison, tell students that the distance around a city block is about $\frac{1}{2}$ mile (0.8 km), which means a cheetah could sprint around the block twice in about 1 minute.

Explain to students that for this activity, they will calculate the median, mode, and mean of data and graph the results. Review the terms *median, mode,* and *mean* with students: *Median* is the middle value of data written in numerical order, *mode* is the value that occurs most often, and *mean* is the average, or sum, of the values divided by the total number of values in the set.

Modeling

Give each student a copy of the **Animal Olympics Data reproducible (page 170).** Display a transparency of the reproducible on the overhead projector. Point out the Fastest Runners data, which includes 11 values presented in random order. Ask students to help you write the values in numerical order, from least to greatest (*40, 42, 42, 43, 45, 47, 47, 50, 50, 55, 70*). By writing the values in numerical order, you can better compare and analyze the data. Ask students, "Now that we have written the values in order, which animal do we clearly see is the fastest runner?" (*cheetah*). "Which animal is the slowest?" (*ostrich*).

Then have students help you calculate the median (47), modes (42, 47, 50), and mean (48.3) of the data. Point out that there are three modes because 42, 47, and 50 all occur twice. Also, the mean can be rounded to the nearest whole number, tenth, or hundredth, whichever is most helpful for analyzing the data. The three measures of central tendency help you predict that the animal with a speed of about 47 or 48 mph (75.64 to 77.25 km/hr) will most likely be in the middle of the pack.

Tell students that you are going to make a bar graph of the data. Ask, "Why would a bar graph be helpful for comparing and analyzing the data?" Explain that a bar graph shows at a glance the relative differences between the runners' speeds. Show students how to set up the bar graph. Point out that you can draw either a vertical or a horizontal graph, with the names of the runners along one axis and the range of speeds along the other.

Think aloud as you decide which range of speeds and increments to include in the number scale. Try different increments (ones, twos, fives, or tens), and point out the pros and cons of each until deciding on increments of fives for the graph. Demonstrate how to graph data by drawing the first two bars as examples.

Guided Practice

Give students copies of the **Animal Olympics Questions** and **Animal Olympics Graph reproducibles (pages 171–172).** Work together as a class to answer the first few questions on the Animal Olympics Questions reproducible. Then gather students into groups of three to complete the remaining problems. Monitor their progress, and refer them to the class examples.

Checking for Understanding

Encourage student groups to share and compare their answers. Ask, "What did the median, mode, and mean tell you about the animals in each race? Why was it helpful to make a bar graph of the data? What conclusions could you reach just by looking at the bar graph? How does the speed of the land runners compare to the swimmers and the jumpers? Which results were the most surprising? Why?" Then tell students that they are going to use what they learned to help them analyze data from a relay race.

Independent Practice

Take students outdoors to complete a 100-meter dash or long jump event. Repeat the activity twice, having partners take turns timing and recording each other's results. Then give students a copy of the class results to graph and interpret for homework. Tell them to write at least three math questions (with answers) about the results. Encourage them to refer to their Animal Olympics Graph as a guide.

Closure

Invite students to share and compare their graphs and math questions about the relay race. Then ask them to answer the following questions in their math journals: "What did you learn from graphing and analyzing the Animal Olympics data? How did that help you to organize and analyze data from the class relay? Why might a real Olympic racer want to keep records of his or her results and compare them with competitors' results?"

Extending the Activity

- Ask students to use the data to create and analyze another type of graph or data plot of their choosing (such as a line plot or a stem-and-leaf plot). Encourage them to use computers to create their graphs or plots.
- Have students research other animals to add to the data and then explain how these new competitors might affect the results of the race.
- Suggest that students go online to research and record the winners of the last five Calaveras Frog Jumping Contests. Have them graph and interpret the results of those jumps.
- Have students compare and analyze data from past Olympic Games. They may go online to research the data or look in reference books such as almanacs.

Animal Olympics Data

Directions: Use these animal data charts to answer the questions on the **Animal Olympics Questions** sheet.

Fastest Runners*

Thomson's gazelle	47 mph (76 km/hr)
Pronghorn antelope	55 mph (89 km/hr)
Springbok	50 mph (80 km/hr)
Cheetah	70 mph (113 km/hr)
Grant's gazelle	47 mph (76 km/hr)
Brown hare	45 mph (72 km/hr)
Greyhound	42 mph (68 km/hr)
Red deer	42 mph (68 km/hr)
Ostrich	40 mph (64 km/hr)
Mongolian gazelle	50 mph (80 km/hr)
Horse	43 mph (69 km/hr)

Fastest Swimmers*

Bluefin tuna	46 mph (74 km/hr)
Sailfish	68 mph (110 km/hr)
Yellowfin tuna	44 mph (70 km/hr)
Blue shark	43 mph (69 km/hr)
Wahoo	41 mph (66 km/hr)
Tiger shark	33 mph (53 km/hr)
Bonefish	40 mph (64 km/hr)
Marlin	50 mph (80 km/hr)
Tarpon	35 mph (56 km/hr)
Swordfish	40 mph (64 km/hr)

Farthest Jumpers*

Red kangaroo	42 ft (13 m)
Thomson's gazelle	30 ft (9 m)
Kangaroo rat	6 ft (2 m)
Jackrabbit	20 ft (6 m)
Frog	21 ft (6 m)

All values are rounded to the nearest whole number.

Name_____   Date_____

Animal Olympics Questions

Directions: Answer these questions using the **Animal Olympics Data** sheet.

1. Which runner would win a 100-meter relay race? _____

2. Which runner would finish last in a 100-meter relay race? _____

3. A cheetah can run 100 meters in about 3 seconds. About
   how long would it take a cheetah to finish a 1,500-meter race? _____

4. A tarpon fish can swim about half as fast as a cheetah can run. About how
   long would it take the tarpon to finish a 100-meter race? 200-meter race?
   800-meter race?
   100 meters: _____ 200 meters: _____ 800 meters: _____

5. About how many jumps does it take a kangaroo
   rat to get as far as a red kangaroo does in one jump? _____

6. If a Thomson's gazelle jumps two times in a row,
   how many jumps will it take for a jackrabbit to catch up? _____

7. Calculate the median, mode, and mean for each data set. Which competitor is most
   likely to be in the middle of the group for each race?

	Median	Mode	Mean	Middle Competitor
Runners				
Swimmers				
Jumpers				

8. Make three different bar graphs, one for each event: Fastest Runners, Fastest
   Swimmers, Farthest Jumpers. Use the **Animal Olympics Graph** sheet to draw each
   graph. Include a title, labels for each axis and bar, and an appropriate number scale.

9. Write one question about your graph. Then exchange papers with a classmate, who
   will answer your question and write his or her own question about the graph. Repeat
   the exchange process with a different classmate for the third question. Be sure to
   check each other's work to make sure it is correct.

Name _____ Date _____

Animal Olympics Graph

Title: _____

Question 1: _____

_____

Answer: _____

Question 2: _____

_____

Answer: _____

Question 3: _____

_____

Answer: _____

Name_____ **Date**_____

Journal Page

1. What did I learn today?

_____

_____

_____

_____

2. How does what I learned connect or add to something I already learned?

_____

_____

_____

_____

3. How can what I learned help me in the future?

_____

_____

_____

_____

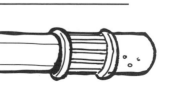

Answer Key

Shopping List Cards (pages 4–5)

1. a. 4, b. 9, c. 36, d. 36

2. a. 5, b. 8, c. 40, d. 40

3. a. 6, b. 5, c. 30, d. 30

4. a. 4, b. 3, c. 24, d. 24

5. a. 8, b. 9, c. 72, d. 72

6. a. 5, b. 4, c. 20, d. 20

7. a. 1, b. 2, c. 6, d. 6

8. a. 9, b. 7, c. 63, d. 63

Guess-timate Estimates (page 12)

1. 480
2. 24,000
3. 5,000
4. 14,000
5. 200
6. 3,600
7. 16,000
8. 240
9. 500
10. 1,500
11. –12. Answers will vary.

Multiplying Multiples (page 15)

Across	Down
5. $80 \times 900 = 72,000$	1. $70 \times 600 = 42,000$
6. $80 \times 700 = 56,000$	2. $400 \times 90 = 36,000$
7. $20 \times 3 = 60$	3. $90 \times 300 = 27,000$
8. $700 \times 40 = 28,000$	4. $30 \times 50 = 1,500$
10. $2 \times 20 = 40$	7. $800 \times 80 = 64,000$
12. $900 \times 50 = 45,000$	9. $90 \times 90 = 8,100$
14. $300 \times 7 = 2,100$	11. $3 \times 30 = 90$
15. $200 \times 60 = 12,000$	13. $6 \times 90 = 540$
17. $20 \times 70 = 1,400$	14. $400 \times 6 = 2,400$
18. $600 \times 30 = 18,000$	16. $3 \times 80 = 240$

200 Catch Game (page 18)

1. 150
2. 100
3. 175
4. –125
5. –200

6. 25

7. −25

8. −50

9. 125

10. 75

11. 200

12. 50

13. Lowest: Kelli

14. Highest: Lisette

Blocks of Division (page 23)

Students should show the steps of long division and picture models (flats, sticks, ones) for each step to get these final answers:

1. $442 \div 3 = 147 \text{ R}1$

2. $375 \div 5 = 75$

Words of Division Chart (page 28)

1. dividend

2. divisor

3. divisible

4. quotient

5. remainder

6. compatible

7. inverse

8. regroup

9. operation

10. equation

Show the Order (page 40)

1. $2 \cdot (6 + 5) - 18 \div 2 + 2^2$

2. Possible answer: $(24 + 8) \div (4 - 2)$

3. $100 \div 2^2 + 3(6 - 2) = 25 + 12 = 37$

4. $112 - (4 \cdot 6) + (3 \cdot 5) \Rightarrow 112 - 24 + 15 \Rightarrow 88 + 15 \Rightarrow 103$ customers

5. $168 - (6 \cdot 5) - (6 \cdot 5 \div 2) - 3(6 \cdot 5 \div 2) - 19 \Rightarrow 168 - (30) - (30 \div 2) - 3(30 \div 2) - 19 \Rightarrow 168 - 30 - 15 - 3(15) - 19 \Rightarrow 168 - 30 - 15 - 45 - 19 \Rightarrow 168 - (30 + 15 + 45 + 19) \Rightarrow 168 - 109 \Rightarrow 59$ meals left

Party Planners Price Chart (page 71)

	Pricing	5 People	10 People	20 People	50 People	100 People
Luxury Dining Hall	$4.00 per person	$20	$40	$80	$200	$400
DJ Music	flat rate	$100/hr	$100/hr	$100/hr	$100/hr	$100/hr
Live Band	flat rate	$200/hr	$200/hr	$200/hr	$200/hr	$200/hr
Party Favors	$2.50 per person	$12.50	$25	$50	$125	$250
*Game Tables	$150 per table (seats 6)	$150 (1 table)	$300 (2 tables)	$600 (4 tables)	$1,350 (9 tables)	$2,550 (17 tables)
Appetizers	$3.50 per person	$17.50	$35	$70	$175	$350
Meat Meal	$19.95 per person	$99.75	$199.50	$399	$997.50	$1,995
Poultry Meal	$12.00 per person	$60	$120	$240	$600	$1,200
Seafood Meal	$15.75 per person	$78.75	$157.50	$315	$787.50	$1,575
Vegetarian Meal	$10.00 per person	$50	$100	$200	$500	$1,000
Buffet Meal	$22.50 per person	$112.50	$225	$450	$1,125	$2,250
Dessert Bar	$7.50 per person	$37.50	$75	$150	$375	$750
Special Drinks	$4.50 per person	$22.50	$45	$90	$225	$450
Photographer	flat rate	$75/hr + $1.50/ photo	$75/hr + $1.50/ photo	$75/hr + $1.50/ photo	$75/hr + $1.50/ photo	$75/hr + $1.50/ photo

Party Planners Reservation List (page 72)

Jones Party (20 people, 1.5 hours)	
	Price
Luxury Dining Hall	$80.00
5 Meat Meals	$99.75
5 Poultry Meals	$60.00
4 Seafood Meals	$63.00
6 Vegetarian Meals	$60.00
Dessert Bar	$150.00
Special Drinks	$90.00
TOTAL	$602.75
20% Deposit	$120.55
Remaining Balance	$482.20

Phan Party (50 people, 2 hours)	
	Price
DJ Music	$200.00
Party Favors	$125.00
Appetizers	$175.00
Buffet Meals	$1,125.00
Dessert Bar	$375.00
Photographer	$150.00
+ 36 Photos	$54.00
TOTAL	$2,204.00
20% Deposit	$440.80
Remaining Balance	$1,763.20

Dominguez Party (100 people, 2 hours)	
	Price
Live Band	$400.00
Game Tables	$2,550.00
Appetizers	$350.00
Buffet Meals	$2,250.00
Dessert Bar	$750.00
Special Drinks	$450.00
Photographer	$150.00
+ 72 Photos	$108.00
TOTAL	$7,008.00
20% Deposit	$1,401.60
Remaining Balance	$5,606.40

Harris Party (400 people, 4 hours)	
	Price
Luxury Dining	$1,600.00
DJ Music	$400.00
Party Favors	$1,000.00
Buffet Meals	$9,000.00
Dessert Bar	$3,000.00
Special Drinks	$1,800.00
Photographer	$300.00
+ 144 Photos	$216.00
TOTAL	$17,316.00
20% Deposit	$3,463.20
Remaining Balance	$13,852.80

Fraction Cooking (page 76)

2 Dozen Muffins: $3\frac{1}{2}$ cups flour, 1 cup brown sugar, 2 tsp. baking powder, $1\frac{1}{2}$ cups skim milk, 2 eggs, 6 Tbs. butter, $2\frac{1}{4}$ cups grated carrots, $\frac{2}{3}$ cup chopped walnuts, 1 tsp. cinnamon

3 Dozen Muffins: $5\frac{1}{4}$ cups flour, $1\frac{1}{2}$ cups brown sugar, 3 tsp. baking powder, $2\frac{1}{4}$ cups skim milk, 3 eggs, 9 Tbs. butter, $3\frac{3}{8}$ cups grated carrots, 1 cup chopped walnuts, $1\frac{1}{2}$ tsp. cinnamon

1. $\frac{9}{12} = \frac{3}{4}$ eggs left

2. $\frac{9}{36} = \frac{1}{4}$ sold

3. Double the amounts

What's Your Angle? (page 86)

1. ∠Q, ∠HQV, ∠VQH (Trace in red.)

2. ∠F, ∠DFL, ∠LFD (Trace in yellow.)

3. ∠W, ∠PWJ, ∠JWP (Trace in blue.)

4. ∠N, ∠XNG, ∠GNX (Trace in yellow.)

5. ∠D, ∠SDR, ∠RDS (Trace in red.)

6. ∠B, ∠MBT, ∠TBM (Trace in blue.)

Triangle Trickster (page 90)

1. right

2. acute

3. obtuse

4. party, triangle

5. equilateral

6. sides, scalene

Answer: Cinderelephant

Trouble at the Tangram Zoo (page 98)

1. cat

2. bear

3. eagle

4. fox

5. duck

6. rabbit

7. flamingo

8. lion

9. swan

10. camel

11. skunk

12. giraffe

Answer: T. rex dinosaur

More Magic Carpets (page 102)

1. $P = 20$ ft	$A = 24$ ft^2
2. $P = 44$ cm	$A = 120$ cm^2
3. $P = 30$ yd	$A = 54$ yd^2
4. $P = 28$ in	$A = 49$ in^2
5. $P = 16$ ft	$A = 15$ ft^2
6. $P = 36$ m	$A = 80$ m^2

From Farm to Factory (page 113–114)

1. About 272 trees; 1 ha = 2.5 acres = 2.5 × 43,560 ft^2 = 108,900 ft^2; so 108,900 ft^2 ÷ 400 ft^2 of land per tree = 272 trees

2. From 27,200 (minimum) to 54,400 (maximum) apples for 272 trees

3. Volume per apple (sphere) = $\frac{4}{3} \pi r^3$ = ($\frac{4}{3}$) (3.14)(1¼)3 = 8.16 in^3 per apple

   Bag: lwh = (6 × 4 × 16) ÷ 8.16 = about 47 apples

   Basket: $\pi r^2 h$ = [(3.14)(9.25)^2 × 8] ÷ 8.16 = about 263 apples

   Carton: lwh = (15 × 12 × 10) ÷ 8.16 = about 221 apples

   Barrel: $\pi r^2 h$ = [(3.14)(12)^2 × 36] ÷ 8.16 = about 1,995 apples

   Bin: lwh = (36 × 40 × 24) ÷ 8.16 = about 4,235 apples

4. 54,400 apples (maximum) ÷ 221 apples per carton = 246.15; round up to 247 cartons

5. 54,400 apples (maximum) × ¼ lb = 54,400 ÷ 4 = 13,600 lb

6. 2 tons per truckload = 4,000 lb, so 13,600 lb of apples ÷ 4,000 = 3.4, so you need about 4 truckloads

7. 13,600 lb of apples × ½ ($3.00) = 13,600 × $1.50 = $20,400 for the entire crop

8. $20,400 ÷ 2 = $10,200 profit

9. Possible answers: The trees produce fewer apples than expected; the amount paid for the apples decreases due to the economy; unexpected events, such as crop damage from weather or pests, causes a decrease.

10. Problems and solutions will vary but should include measurements of apples or containers of apples.

Just Simplify! (page 120)

1. 25
2. 30
3. 40
4. 60
5. 20
6. 40
7. 18
8. 82
9. 38
10. 12

Equal—or *Not!* (page 123)

1. =
2. =
3. ≠
4. ≠

5. ≠

6. =

7. =

8. ≠

9. =

10. ≠

Sunken Treasure (page 129)

1. b: 8, 9, 10, 11

2. a: 2, 4, 6, 8

3. d: 20, 18, 16, 14

4. b: 8, 11, 12, 17

5. b: 20, 15, 10, 5

6. d: 10, 11, 12, 13

7. 10

8. 18

9. 20

10. 13

Out of This World (page 138)

1. 25

2. 10

3. pickle and garlic

4. oyster

5. pizza

6. 15

Project Reading (page 141)

1. 105

2. 75

3. *The Secret Garden*

4. *Treasure Island*

5. 75

6. 105

Ants, Ants, Ants! (page 145)

1. restaurant

2. school

3. (2,9)

4. (0,5)

5. (5,4)

6. 0, 10, 3

7. 0, 6, 7

8. 0, 9, 5

Fast Food Comparisons: Part 1 (page 155)

Hamburgers (Regular: 250, 270, 280, 280, 320; Special: 410, 550, 590, 590, 680)

1. Regular = median 280, mode 280, mean 280, range 70

2. Specialty = median 590, mode 590, mean 564, range 270

Chicken (Regular: 290, 300, 400, 450, 550; Club: 470, 470, 520, 550, 740)

3. Regular = median 400, mode (none), mean 398, range 260

4. Club = median 520, mode 470, mean 550, range 270

French Fries (Small: 210, 230, 270, 290, 350; Large: 570, 600, 610, 610, 620)

5. Small = median 270, mode (none), mean 270, range 140

6. Large = median 610, mode 610, mean 602, range 50

Salads (Garden: 50, 100, 110; Chicken: 100, 200, 200)

7. Garden = median 100, mode (none), mean ~87, range 60

8. Chicken = median 200, mode 200, mean ~167, range 100

Drinks (Small: 160, 160, 160; Medium: 220, 220, 230; Large: 320, 320, 330)

9. Small = median 160, mode 160, mean 160, range 0

10. Medium = mean 220, mode 220, mean ~223, range 10

11. Large = median 320, mode 320, mean ~323, range 10

Fast Food Comparisons: Part 2 (page 156)

All answers were determined using the mean:

1. Possible answers: Regular Hamburger Meal = 280 + 270 + 160 = 710 total cal

2. Specialty Hamburger Meal = 564 + 602 + 323 = 1,489 total cal

3. Regular Chicken Meal = 398 + 270 + 160 = 828 total cal

4. Chicken Club Meal = 550 + 602 + 323 = 1,475 total cal

5. –8. Answers will vary but should include the correct calories listed for "extras" below the food charts.

9. Answers will vary but may include these comparisons: The calories for small and large fries are about the same as the calories for regular and specialty hamburgers. The regular chicken meal is higher in calories than the regular hamburger meal. The specialty hamburger meal is more than twice the calories of a regular hamburger meal. By adding extras, you might double or even triple the calories of your food.

Fast Food Comparisons: Part 3 (page 157)

Ages 7–10: Boys ~657 cal per meal; Girls 580 cal per meal

Ages 11–14: Boys 740 cal per meal; Girls ~617 cal per meal

Ages 15–18: Boys 920 cal per meal; Girls ~703 cal per meal

Answers will vary, depending on added extras. Sample answers for 10-year-old boy and meals without extras are as follows. All answers were determined using the mean:

Regular Hamburger Meal: 710 cal for meal; 53 cal > needed cal per meal; $(710 \div 1,970) \times 100 = 36\%$ daily cal

Specialty Hamburger Meal: 1,489 cal for meal; 832 cal > needed cal per meal; $(1,489 \div 1,970) \times 100 = 76\%$ daily cal

Regular Chicken Meal: 828 cal for meal; 171 cal > needed cal per meal; $(828 \div 1,970) \times 100 = 42\%$ daily cal

Chicken Club Meal: 1,475 cal for meal; 818 cal > needed cal per meal; $(1,475 \div 1,970) \times 100 = 75\%$ daily cal

Answers will vary. Sample answers: Fast food meals often have more calories than needed to maintain a healthy body. You can reduce the amount of calories from fast foods by not consuming fries, sodas, and extras. Healthier alternatives might include eating salads at fast food restaurants, with limited or no salad dressing, or just bypassing eating out and opting for preparing fresh, balanced meals at home.

Animal Olympics Questions (page 171)

1. cheetah

2. ostrich

3. About 45 sec

4. 100 m = 6 sec, 200 m = 12 sec, 800 m = 48 sec

5. 7 jumps

6. 3 jumps

7. **Runners** (40, 42, 42, 43, 45, 47, 47, 50, 50, 55, 70): median = 47; modes = 42, 47, 50; mean = 48.3; middle competitor = Thomson's gazelle or Grant's gazelle

   Swimmers (33, 35, 40, 40, 41, 43, 44, 46, 50, 68): median = (41 + 43) ÷ 2 = 42; mode = 40; mean = 44; middle competitor = yellowfin tuna

   Jumpers (6, 20, 21, 30, 42): median = 21; mode = none; mean = 23.8; middle competitor = frog

8. Check students' graphs to make sure they are drawn correctly and accurately according to the data.

9. Answers will vary but should relate to students' graphs.

Resources

About.com. (2008). *Card game rules: Spoons.* Retrieved February 6, 2008, from http://boardgames.about.com/od/cardgames/a/spoons.htm

Ash, R. (1999). *The top ten of everything 2000.* New York: DK.

Bamberger, H., & Hughes, P. (1995). *Super graphs, venns, and glyphs.* New York: Scholastic Professional Books.

Easy Calculation.com. (n.d.). *Volume conversion table.* Retrieved December 15, 2007, from http://www.easycalculation.com/unit-conversion/volume-factors.php

EZ Calculators. (2006). *Area conversion calculator.* Retrieved December 15, 2007, from http://www.ez-calculators.com/area_conversion_calculator.htm

Farmington Fresh LLC. (2006). *Whole round apple packing.* Retrieved December 18, 2007, from http://www.farmfresh.com/wra_packaging.php

Fast Food.com. (2004). *Fast food nutrition: Calorie guide!* Retrieved January 3, 2008, from http://www.fastfood.com/nutrition

Highline Advanced Math Program. (n.d.). *Math term definition.* Retrieved January 15, 2008, from http://home.avvanta.com/~math/def2.cgi?t=1cm

Houghton Mifflin. (2002). *Mathematics: California edition.* Boston: Houghton Mifflin.

Kellow, J. (2007, December 20). *Good nutrition for children.* Retrieved January 5, 2008, from http://www.weightlossresources.co.uk/children/nutrition_calorie_needs.htm

Kimble-Ellis, S. (1997). *Math puzzlers.* New York: Scholastic Professional Books.

Mathematische Basteleien. (n.d.). *Fortune teller.* Retrieved January 7, 2008, from http://www.mathematische-basteleien.de/fortune_teller.htm

Miller, M., & Lee, M. (1997). *The mega-fun multiplication facts activity book.* New York: Scholastic Professional Books.

National Council of Teachers of Mathematics. (2005). *Principles and standards for school mathematics.* Reston, VA: Author.

National Council of Teachers of Mathematics. (2008). *Curriculum focal points for prekindergarten through grade 8 mathematics: Grade 4.* Retrieved December 18, 2007, from http://www.nctm.org/standards/focalpoints.aspx?id=330&ekmensel=c580fa7b_10_52_330_5

New York Public Library. (1998). *The New York Public Library desk reference* (3rd ed.). New York: Stonesong Press.

Nielsen, B. (2008). *Tangrammer.* Retrieved February 7, 2008, from http://www.246.dk/tandata.html

PBS Kids. (n.d.). *Sagwa: Games: Tangrams.* Retrieved February 7, 2008, from http://pbskids.org/sagwa/games/tangrams/index.html

Piccirilli, R. (1996). *Write about math!* New York: Scholastic Professional Books.

Sousa, D. A. (2006). *How the brain learns* (3rd ed.). Thousand Oaks, CA: Corwin.

Sousa, D. A. (2008). *How the brain learns mathematics.* Thousand Oaks, CA: Corwin.

CORWIN
A SAGE Company

The Corwin logo—a raven striding across an open book—represents the union of courage and learning. Corwin is committed to improving education for all learners by publishing books and other professional development resources for those serving the field of PreK–12 education. By providing practical, hands-on materials, Corwin continues to carry out the promise of its motto: **"Helping Educators Do Their Work Better."**